VICTORY BETRAYED

OPERATION DEWEY CANYON STANDS AS A DECISIVE
VICTORY OVER COMMUNIST FORCES, AS WELL AS A
TESTAMENT TO THE INGENUITY AND AUDACITY OF
MARINE CORPS LEADERS, THE EFFECTIVENESS OF THE
MARINE AIR/GROUND TEAM, AND THE TENACITY OF
MARINES IN BATTLE.

RONALD WINTER

D1522657

Spectre Communications
www.RonaldWinterBooks.com

Mid-Continent Public Library
15616 East US Highway 24
Independence, MO 64050

VICTORY BETRAYED

For information about **Spectre Communications**

Please visit our website at www.RonaldWinterBooks.com

Email: RWinterBooks@comcast.net

Winter, Ronald,
VICTORY BETRAYED/ Ronald Winter
ISBN 13: 978-1-7348369-0-5
Non-Fiction, Military

First Published by **Spectre Communications** in the USA

May 2020

10 9 8 7 6 5 4 3 2 1

Printed in the USA

FOREWORD

Jay Standish, Capt. USMC
2nd Battalion, 9th Marines
Operation Dewey Canyon

Operation Dewey Canyon is one of the largest and most successful Marine Corps operations of the Vietnam War. To avoid criticism, Washington did not want to admit that during the operation the US made a major—and successful—incursion into Laos and temporarily cut off the Ho Chi Minh Trail. The details were shrouded in secrecy until many years later.

The A Shau Valley, where Dewey Canyon was fought, was a notorious NVA stronghold south of Khe Sanh and adjacent to the Laotian border, providing sanctuary, a major supply base, and a main route of the Ho Chi Minh Trail. The Valley was known to Marines in I Corps as well fortified, a base for large NVA units, and the most dangerous area in I Corps—a very "bad ass" place. Never previously penetrated by large US units, it was only spied on by small Marine Force Recon teams at huge risk and sometimes ruin.

Victory Betrayed provides the details of the battle, in the words of Dewey Canyon veterans, and shows how it was one of the few US campaigns that was strategic in concept and execution. The other was the 1972 Christmas Bombing of Hanoi and Haiphong by waves of B-52's which, in just 11 days, nearly destroyed the enemy's strategic infrastructure in the North, forcing them back to the peace table.

During Dewey Canyon—with Presidential approval—an entire regiment of 5000 Marines (9th Marine Regiment) formed on line. An entire battalion crossed the border into Laos, cutting the Trail, and overrunning the enemy, killing many communist forces while capturing one of the largest hauls of weapons and supplies in the war.

Years later, the NVA General who managed the Trail admitted that if the US cut and held the Trail for a longer period, the North could not have resupplied their troops and sustained the war.

This is the story of the brave men of the 9th Marines, who defeated a well-entrenched enemy on their home base, and, for a week, cut one of their major supply routes, providing a blueprint for winning the Vietnam War that was ignored and even opposed by officials in the US.

It is one of the most inspiring chapters of Marine Corps History.

Dedication

To Col. Harvey "Barney" Barnum,
E Battery, 2nd Battalion, 12th Marines, Medal of Honor Recipient,
and to the Memory of James L. Johnson,
E Company, 2nd Battalion, 9th Marines, Navy Cross Recipient
Marines' Marines.

And to all the ground pounders, cannon cockers and wing wipers
who engaged the NVA in the A Shau Valley
and along the Ho Chi Minh Trail and emerged victorious!

Semper Fidelis!

VICTORY BETRAYED

Prologue

To fully grasp the importance of Operation Dewey Canyon, an overwhelming, though hard-fought victory by the 9th Marine Regiment and supporting units against the communist North Vietnamese in early 1969, we must step back and view the situation from an eagle's perspective.

From a global standpoint, the argument could be made that Vietnam was actually a diversion—a massive, long-lasting and costly diversion to be sure—but a diversion, nonetheless. The reason for this supposition is that Vietnam was not the primary goal in Southeast Asia for either the communists or free-world forces.

That distinction falls to the Straits of Malacca, a narrow waterway that runs between Indonesia and Malaysia. It is the most direct route from eastern Africa, India and other southern Asian countries to the South China Sea. Natural geographical barriers channel a huge portion of the world's sea bound trade through this strait. In modern times 90 percent of all world trade goes by ship, and of that amount, 50 percent uses the Straits of Malacca and the South China Sea.[1]

Even within the past decade fully half of the total seaborne trade tonnage still goes through the strait, making it the primary chokepoint for international trade.[2] A significant percentage of this trade is oil, on its way to fuel the economies of Pacific Rim countries. Controlling the strait could make trade among capitalist countries extraordinarily difficult, dangerous, and far more costly.

VICTORY BETRAYED — Ronald Winter

In post-World War II geo-political maneuvering, communist forces zeroed in on three major chokepoints to ocean-going trade—the Panama Canal, the Suez Canal and the Straits of Malacca. Several other chokepoints matter on a regional level, including the Bosphorous and Dardanelles straits. These straits control access between the Black Sea and the Aegean, and ultimately the Mediterranean. Also, the Straits of Hormuz see 20 percent of the world's oil on a daily basis, but control of international shipping rests with control of the Panama and Suez Canals, and the Straits of Malacca.

By 1960, Fidel Castro controlled Cuba and was exporting troops and political cadre to Central America and northern South America, putting the Panama Canal in jeopardy. Russia cozied up to the Egyptians, who control the Suez Canal. Communists gained extraordinary influence over Indonesia's Prime Minister Sukarno, who exported communist troops across the strait to fight in Malaysia where a major insurgency was underway. Communist control of both Indonesia and Malaysia meant control of the Straits of Malacca, causing a serious crimp in the shipping trade.

Malaysian government forces, aided by British, Australian, New Zealand, Thai, South Vietnamese, and American units fought the communists since 1948. Members of Malaysia's huge ethnic Chinese minority fought in the communist offensive. Fighting slowed in Malaysia by 1960. Yet, in the coming decade, the situation in Indonesia grew dire.[3]

This tenuous environment combined with the escalating fighting in South Vietnam, placed the region in danger of falling to communist forces. The United States acted by supporting anti-communist forces in Indonesia. Since Indonesia was and is a Muslim country the population and the military were agitated over the extraordinary influence the communists had on Sukarno. Agitation erupted in 1965, with Sukarno barely surviving a coup attempt.

VICTORY BETRAYED — Ronald Winter

Nonetheless, by 1966 General Suharto replaced Sukarno and ultimately became the country's leader. While the history of who initiated the coup depends on who is telling it, the result is that Suharto survived by gaining the confidence of Sukarno. One version of those long-ago events is that Suharto—allegedly one of the coup plotters—hearing that the coup had been revealed, ran *to* the sounds of the guns, rather than away *from* them. He headed right to the royal palace where he convinced Sukarno that he wanted to help him.

Within the next year, Suharto replaced Sukarno in office and initiated a massive anti-communist offensive, spearheaded by the military and aided by the CIA. That offensive continued for the next three years and killed 500,000 communists. While British and other Commonwealth forces fought the communists in Malaysia, the situation in Indonesia became a full military conflagration. In contrast, Malaysia stabilized.

As the situation in Indonesia exploded, the number of US forces in Vietnam increased exponentially on the heels of the Gulf of Tonkin resolution in 1964. The allied involvement in South Vietnam proceeded apace with the fighting in Indonesia, with very similar results. Yet, in Indonesia the communists had no means of reinforcement and resupply. At the same time in South Vietnam, the north sent troops and materiel south on the Ho Chi Minh Trail, with little effective resistance.

By 1969, even if the US withdrew from South Vietnam, the communists would still have a very difficult time traversing the remainder of Southeast Asia to Malaysia and south to the straits. Communist guerillas continued to operate in northern Malaysia for years to come. Their efforts were unsuccessful, but they withdrew from the field only when the Soviet Union collapsed.

All these factors combined into the world view in the 1960s

and into the 1970s. Across the region communist forces took a horrible beating. Nonetheless, when Saigon fell on April 30, 1975, it became fashionable to blame the loss of South Vietnam on the American military. The media still blames the American military to this day. Politicians avoid the issue in public, although some privately repeat that mantra even at symposia questioning "What the Military Did Wrong in Vietnam."

But is the fall of South Vietnam really the fault of the military? A better question is, how can the fall of South Vietnam be the fault of the military when US forces won every single major battle they fought with the communists? The United States lost 58,000 troops—48,000 in battle, and 10,000 due to illnesses and accidents. The communists admitted to losing between 1.1 million[4] and 1.5 million troops, out of a total of 3 million Vietnamese killed on both sides in the war.[5] Stunningly, the Communists never won a single major engagement against the US. This includes a significant communist defeat at the hands of South Vietnamese ground units, supported by US air, in the Easter Invasion of 1972. It wasn't until the very last battle in 1975 that limited US forces joined at the last minute to evacuate US personnel and a few allies. Then and only then could the communists claim victory.

But even as late in the war as Easter 1972—when an estimated 250,000 northern troops, including massive armored and artillery divisions, invaded with the intent of overthrowing the south while US advisers were still "in country"—the military side of the equation tilted heavily toward the US and its allies. Intelligence sources say the communists lost between 75,000 and 150,000 troops killed in action in the Easter 1972 invasion. The defeat so overwhelmed the north that the famed communist General, Vo Nguyen Giap, who is credited with defeating the French in post-World War II fighting, was fired and placed under house arrest for the next three years.

This is not to say that free-world forces had an easy go of it during the Vietnam War. Many of the battles were brutal. The US and its allies often were seriously outnumbered by communist forces, especially in the early years of the war. But even without numeric parity, the combination of US firepower exercised by infantry and artillery, backed by air power and naval gunfire, was far and away superior to the communists.

So, how did the Vietnamese communists manage to stay involved through 15 years of warfare that devastated their population? At about 20 million citizens, North Vietnam was roughly one-tenth the size of the US population at that time.[6] For US losses to have been equal to the North Vietnamese, we would have had to lose between 11 million and 15 million troops, killed in action, not wounded or total casualties. That's 11-15 million killed in action. Put in that perspective, the communists took horrendous losses, but were still able to send supplies and reinforcements to their units in the south, and therein lies the secret of their success.

Communism's core philosophy is that the state is all-important and all powerful, that the rights of the individual don't exist when aligned against the state. The communists had no issue with the numbers of their losses, so long as the communist bosses in Hanoi, Beijing (Peking) and Moscow got what they wanted in the long run. So, despite defeat after defeat at the hands of free-world forces, the north continued to resupply and reinforce—at times even using Russian mercenaries[7] and especially communist Chinese replacements.[8]

They did this primarily along the Ho Chi Minh Trail, as routes that had been available across the Demilitarized Zone (DMZ) early in the war, were blocked by allied forces. Due to patrolling by the US Navy and Coast Guard, as well as the South Vietnamese Navy, sea routes simply did not exist on the level that was necessary to keep the communist army in the mix.

Ultimately, the communists—abroad and in the US—were able to whittle away at the will of the US Congress, or clandestinely support the election of Representatives and Senators who shared their beliefs. By the 1970s, American media was pro-communist and anti-capitalist, and actively assisted the communist forces by flat out lying about Western military successes. The voting power in the US Congress swung far enough onto the communist side to muster sufficient votes to withdraw support from South Vietnam.

Within two years of the signing of the Paris Peace Accords in January 1973, that supposedly ended the war with a peace agreement, the US Congress voted twice to isolate and abandon South Vietnam. These decisions left the South Vietnamese government and millions of Southeast Asian citizens to their horrendous fate.

In the meantime, the communists continued to play the one hand the US State Department gave them at the outset of the war—free access to travel and move supplies down the Ho Chi Minh Trail. The trail started out as little more than jungle paths, but ended up being a sophisticated transportation system that was moving an estimated 1,000 trucks per day full of war supplies, in addition to legions of conscripted communist troops, who knew—as they marched to the war in the south—that there was a good chance they would never go home again.

For this, the US and its allies can thank the signatories to the International Agreement on Laotian Neutrality which was signed by 14 communist and free world countries on July 23, 1962. Literally from the outset, this alleged agreement gave US diplomats a face-saving document that the communists ignored before the ink was dry. In fact, in the early months of 1962—prior to the signing of the agreement—the communists went on a rampage in Laos. Royal Laotian forces were driven across the breadth of their country by the Pathet Lao communists, aided to a huge extent by North Vietnamese forces backed by Russians and Chinese.

VICTORY BETRAYED — Ronald Winter

The situation became dire, with Royal Laotian units retreating across the Mekong River to Thailand. The Kennedy Administration activated a Joint Task Force (JTF 116) of Navy, Marines, Army and Air Force personnel to make the point that Thailand, a member of the Southeast Asia Treaty Organization, (SEATO) was off limits.[9] Ironically, the 3rd Battalion, 9th Marine Regiment embarked as an infantry component that arrived in Udorn, Thailand in mid-June.[10] The US clearly showed that it could mobilize a significant blocking force to thwart communist advances, and do it quickly. But the primary point of all that activity was that it occurred in Thailand, not in Laos and not in Vietnam.

More to the point, with the signing of the agreement of Laotian neutrality, the Kennedy Administration withdrew the entire task force from Thailand. However, two years later, US Air Force squadrons were stationed at Udorn and four other air bases in Thailand, where they provided air support in Southeast Asia through the end of the war. After the US removed its forces from Thailand in 1962, it paid scant attention to Laos, other than CIA support and resupply missions. The communist North Vietnamese solidified their hold on eastern Laos and began infiltrating troops and war materiel to fight on two fronts. And the US turned a blind eye to the flagrant violations of an international agreement, thus permitting the continued supply of the communist war effort right through its final invasion of South Vietnam in 1975.

Nearly seven years after the neutrality pact was signed, the 9th Marines again confronted the North Vietnamese, Chinese, and Russians on the Laotian border, only this time the border was with South Vietnam, not Thailand. However, after the Marines successfully crushed the communists, and briefly took possession of their supply route, the American government upended their efforts, and wrapped the true story of Operation Dewey Canyon so tightly in its web of secrecy that only now—more than a half-century later—are some of these secrets finally seeing daylight.

OVER THE LINE

"The 9th Marines also destroyed thousands of tons of food and medical supplies, even crossing the border from South Vietnam into Laos – legally, but politically incorrect, as it turned out – to accomplish their mission."

Operation Dewey Canyon was fought in the northern I Corps area of South Vietnam and Laos in early 1969. That battle—defined in relation to World War II Marine Corps battles in the Pacific—would include the isolation of Guadalcanal, the miserable terrain, weather and vegetation of Bougainville, an entrenched enemy similar to Pelilu, and the strategic importance of Iwo Jima.

Most WWII Marine battles were fought by division-sized forces that often outnumbered the enemy. Dewey Canyon was fought by the 9th Marine Regiment, consisting of the 1st, 2nd and 3rd Battalions. These battalions were more often than not under-strength and undersupplied. Even when augmented by air power and the artillery of the 2nd Battalion, 12th Marines, the Marines who fought in Dewey Canyon numbered only a fraction of the Marine forces that fought enemy units in previous wars.

Yet, they prevailed.

The battlefield was the upper A Shau Valley, south of Khe Sanh, where it meets the Da Krong River and its valley, a mountainous, jungled region adjacent to a communist sanctuary referred to as Base Area 611. Despite its remote location and the virtually impassible condition of two old roads built decades earlier by the French, Base Area 611 was used by the North Vietnamese communists to mass troops and supplies prior to attacks on the cities of northern I Corps (pronounced *Eye Core*). There the communist forces created underground storage areas and support facilities, including hospitals, that were not only impossible to detect from the air, but often could withstand direct hits from bombs and artillery. Even worse from the American point of view, was that Base Area 611 was located across the border in Laos and was off limits to free-world forces.

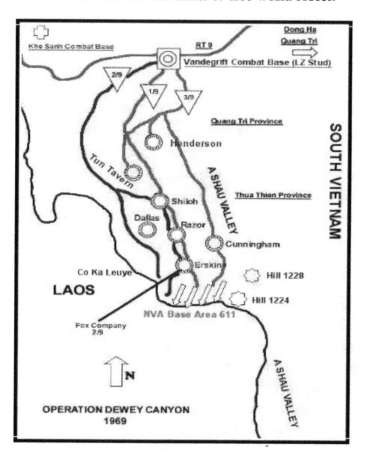

**Figure 1. Dewey Canyon Area of Operations.
(Public Domain)**

Nonetheless, the 9th Marines and supporting forces, including a 2nd Battalion, 3rd Marines security detachment, and an Army of the Republic of Vietnam (ARVN) artillery unit and accompanying infantry, prevailed overwhelmingly against a determined, highly mobile, extremely well-equipped and supplied North Vietnamese communist force. The 9th Marines not only routed opposing communist forces, they disrupted infiltration routes, demolished sophisticated communication systems, and captured or destroyed thousands of weapons intended for use by the enemy in planned spring offensives later that year. The 9th Marines also destroyed thousands of tons of food and medical supplies, even crossing the border from South Vietnam into Laos—legally, but politically incorrect, as it turned out—to accomplish their mission. They took control of a limited section of the Ho Chi Minh trail for the better part of a week—an unprecedented action—and defeated the communists in battle on their home turf throughout the operation. When all was said and done, the number of communists killed officially was listed at 1,617 as confirmed by body count. Many who served on Dewey Canyon believe the actual number of communist troops killed was far higher. But with bodies dragged away into the nearly impenetrable jungle by retreating NVA, or obliterated by direct hits from massive artillery and air strikes, it was impossible to give an accurate count of the destruction levied on the North Vietnamese Army. By contrast, 130 Marines, roughly the equivalent of three platoons or more than half of a full-strength company, were killed in action. An additional 920 wounds were recorded, with many Marines suffering multiple injuries over the course of the operation, but often returning to the battle. The number of communists killed in action, even using the official body count, exceeded the Marine dead by more than 12 times—a devastating blow to an army that was losing all its battles and seeing a steady erosion of its armed forces.

Operation Dewey Canyon, which itself built on the successes of previous operations by the 9th and virtually every other Marine regiment in Vietnam, was eminently successful in achieving its goals and more. The 9th Marines hit the enemy during the monsoons, disrupting preparations for the coming dry season offensive, and crippling the communists' capabilities before the offensive could be launched. It took the initiative away from the communist forces and robbed them of their weaponry, medicine and supplies. In addition to rendering combat ineffective portions of three communist regiments, the tons of food, medicine, ammunition, firearms, artillery, mines and even livestock captured or destroyed were simply astounding. The discovered and destroyed facilities were an integral part of the communist plans for the coming offensive, without which, the North Vietnamese were left adrift. Their spring offensive never materialized and the 9th Marines added Dewey Canyon to the long list of successful Marine operations in Vietnam—with the exception that it was to be the last of the major operations before the beginning of troop withdrawals ordered by President Richard Nixon.

Revisionist historians would later say that the operation was not successful in halting the flow of supplies and manpower down the Ho Chi Minh Trail.[11] But in reality, that was never the task or objective of the operation. The primary purpose of Operation Dewey Canyon was to kill the enemy and deny him supplies, and to block access to the densely populated areas of the coastal lowlands.[12] In that regard, Operation Dewey Canyon stands as a decisive victory over communist forces, as well as a testament to the ingenuity and audacity of Marine Corps leaders, the effectiveness of the Marine air/ground team, and the tenacity of Marines in battle.

AUTHOR'S OBSERVATIONS

Trigger Time

For helicopter crews, reconnaissance team insertions and extractions were a time of high stress and better than average chances of contact with enemy forces. The teams were always inserted in remote locations, and often as not the NVA troops were using that remoteness to screen their infiltration efforts. It was not unusual to insert a team, take off for the next mission and within minutes receive word that the team was *"compromised,"* and asking for an emergency extraction.

Such extractions required consummate flying skills on the part of the pilots and pinpoint fire from the helicopters' gunners to avoid hitting friendly troops, who usually were unseen in jungles or grasslands until the instant the helicopter landed for the extraction. Often, the NVA were listening in on the teams' radio transmissions. Thus, coded messages, devised on the spot, had to be employed. In more than one instance if the communists could hear the pilots telling the team to "Pop a Smoke," meaning a colored smoke grenade that would mark team's position, they would pop a smoke of the same color hoping to draw the helicopter to the wrong location.

For the gunners, these meant almost certain engagements, which were translated in the vernacular of that generation to *"Trigger time!"* As a gunner, trigger time was often the adrenaline-induced highlight of my day.

IN THE BEGINNING

"At one o'clock I assembled the staff and commanders.
Before dark, battalion positions had become company positions.
It happened just that fast."

Enemy activity throughout northern I Corps was light and sporadic during the early days of January 1969. Along the Demilitarized Zone, units of the 3rd Marine Division and the US Army's 1st Brigade, 5th Infantry Division (Mechanized) faced elements of six battle-hardened North Vietnamese regiments, the <u>138th</u>, <u>270th</u>, <u>84th</u>, <u>31st</u>, <u>27th</u>, and the <u>126th Naval Sappers</u>. Three regiments of the veteran but battered <u>320th NVA Division</u> had withdrawn from western and central Quang Tri Province for refitting in North Vietnam following repeated defeats in 1968. Enemy activity was generally limited to infrequent rocket and mortar attacks on allied positions, ground probes by squad- and platoon-sized units and attempts at interdicting the Song Cua Viet (Cua Viet River) with mines. Artillery fire from within and north of the Demilitarized Zone that garnered constant US media attention in 1967 and early 1968, had all but ceased in December.[13] The DMZ was intended to separate South Vietnam from North Vietnam. In truth, the DMZ merely set a line of demarcation where allied forces were not allowed to pass while the communists ignored it. Free-world armies were not allowed to send a force larger than squad-sized into the DMZ, while communist units of all sizes violated the zone with alacrity.[14]

Nonetheless, since arriving in Vietnam nearly four years earlier and staking out I Corps as its territory, US Marine Corps regiments and supporting arms steadily decimated enemy forces, even during the bitter battles from 1965 through early 1968. During much of that time, Secretary of Defense Robert McNamara ordered Marine units along the DMZ to remain tied down to fixed bases which were part of his Strong Point Obstacle System, better known as The McNamara Line. The SPOS was a series of defenses intended to run from the South China Sea to the Laotian border, based on the ill-fated Maginot Line built by the French to (unsuccessfully) deter German forces in WWII. It was never finished further than a few miles inland at Con Thien, a former French fort and part of Leatherneck Square, a sector of Marine responsibility further outlined by Gio Linh, Dong Ha and Cam Lo.

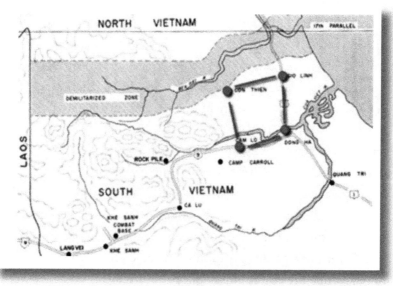

Figure 3. Leatherneck Square outlines 1967.

VICTORY BETRAYED — Ronald Winter

By using cleared land, fencing, artillery, air support, mines, and naval gunfire in addition to Marine combat regiments, the goal of the SPOS was to prevent infiltration from the northern communists, who used the DMZ as a staging area for artillery attacks and infiltration. But the flaw in McNamara's plan was that he didn't want to commit the necessary troops to both clear the land and install the barriers, while simultaneously maintaining the necessary infantry patrols and offensive efforts. This egregious flaw was well-known and documented by Marine officers who were tasked with keeping North Vietnamese forces at bay. But their concerns were literally ignored by the Washington D.C., politicians and bureaucrats. Thus, Marine infantry regiments were forced to remain huddled down in defensive positions which basically only protected the anchors of Leatherneck Square.[15] This gave the NVA the opportunity and ability to pinpoint Marine positions and put the infantry under nearly constant, and horrendous, artillery fire, similar to the static lines of WWI. Regardless, the Marines were largely successful in preventing large scale incursions across that portion of the DMZ, although the NVA countered simply by shifting their supply lines west, expanding the Ho Chi Minh Trail, and entering South Vietnam in the isolated areas further south. US ground forces could not enter what free-world countries considered Laos. To do so would violate the Declaration on Laotian Neutrality signed by both communist and free nations in July 1962. Although the US and other western governments still honored the agreement, communist forces flaunted their refusal to abide by its conditions. In fact, North Vietnam annexed that portion of Laos in late 1958 and early 1959 and considered it part of their country, not a separate political entity. Since that time the Vietnamese communists physically occupied segments of eastern Laos, and governed the occupied areas administratively as well, with the North Vietnamese flag flying over much of the occupied territory.[16] Those early incursions into what had been Laos ultimately gave the communist forces untouchable sanctuaries to which they could retreat and recuperate from their losses when they were being hammered by US forces.[17]

By the time Dewey Canyon was launched, the communists had turned the Ho Chi Minh Trail in Laos and Cambodia into a sophisticated supply line. It was maintained by heavy equipment and used by up to 1,000 trucks per day[18] to move mountains of supplies and hundreds of thousands of troops, in addition to heavy artillery and tracked vehicles, including tanks, into South Vietnam. The network of roads was regularly bombed by US air forces and artillery but was rarely even seen by most allied fighters on the South Vietnam side. Thus, the allies were forced to wait for the communists to show up in the south before engaging them. This they did on virtually every occasion with a ferocity that left the communist forces mauled and retreating to their sanctuaries in North Vietnam and Cambodia, as well as Laos. However, unlike their American counterparts, communist leaders in North Vietnam seemed to have no concern with the magnitude of their losses and continued to send thousands of troops into the South Vietnamese meat grinder. Despite the overwhelming allied victory over communist forces in the 1968 Tet Offensive in February, and the losses of massive numbers of communist troops at Khe Sanh and the Battle for Hue City, through March 1968, media reports so completely misrepresented the situation in Vietnam, that new commanders soon were on the scene. The post-Tet shakeup included the replacement of Army General William Westmoreland, whose deputy, Creighton Abrams soon took over as the top military commander in Vietnam. In May 1968, the 3rd Marine Division in Quang Tri saw a change of command ceremony that brought in Major General Raymond G. "Razor" Davis, a veteran of the Guadalcanal, Cape Gloucester, and Peleliu campaigns of

World War II, and Medal of Honor recipient for heroism at the Chosin Reservoir during the Korean War.[19]

After working briefly with the 101st Airborne, and studying that unit's airmobile tactics,[20] Davis combined his observations with Marine helicopter support tactics as they had been applied since the earliest days of US involvement in Vietnam. During his time in Korea, Marine helicopter units first applied the concept of vertical warfare. The concept of mobility the Marine Corps so effectively used nearly a generation earlier was reintroduced in Vietnam.[21]

Davis took command of the division in May 1968 and immediately took the infantry units out of defense and put them on offense. Prior to Davis' arrival, Marine forces were deployed with battalions often under operational control of different regiments. Most infantry regimental commanders preferred to have their own organic battalions, which provided clear-cut chains of command, while avoiding misconceptions between operational control and administrative command. One regimental commander estimated that it took about two weeks of working with a new battalion to iron out problems of procedures and communications.[22]

As General Davis noted: *"We had something like two dozen battalions up there all tied down (with little exception) to these fixed positions, and the situation didn't demand it. The way to get it done was to get out of these fixed positions and get mobility, to go and destroy the enemy on our terms—not sit there and absorb the shot and shell and frequent penetrations that he was able to mount. So, ... as soon as I heard that I was going, it led me to ... move in prepared in the first hours to completely turn the command upside down. The relief of CGs took place at eleven o'clock. At one o'clock I assembled the staff and commanders. Before dark, battalion positions had become company positions. It happened just that fast."* [23]

Extending this high mobility concept to the whole 3rd Marine

Division, General Davis laid down some ground rules. Unit integrity would be reestablished. Not only would organic battalions work with their parent regiments, but this would also apply to normal support units, particularly direct support artillery. Non-essential combat bases and strong points would be closed, and those that were not closed would be made defendable by no more than one reinforced company. The reconnaissance effort was also to be upgraded, with from 30 to 35 teams to be in the field at all times.[24]

Miles Davis, then a 2nd Lieutenant who would join his famous father on the Dewey Canyon battlefield, recalled his father's assumption of command as a *"jaw-dropping"* moment. Commanders in place in northern I Corps had not seen such rapid changes in tactics in their tours, but Major Gen. Davis was firm and by the end of the day, Marines were breaking out of their politically enforced defensive positions and going on the offense.[25] In addition to establishing a more mobile posture, Davis reinstituted unit integrity.[26] Thus, as Colonel Robert H. Barrow, regimental commander of the 9th Marines, and later Commandant of the Marine Corps, noted, the individual battalions *"had felt . . . they were commanded by strangers. Every unit has a kind of personality of its own, often reflecting the personality of the commander, so you never got to know who did what best, or who would you give this mission to."* Davis changed that. Each regiment, under normal operating circumstances, would now control its constituent battalions. As Davis later commented, *"it was the key to our success."*[27] As battalions of the division moved from defensive operations to more aggressive operations against elements of the 320th NVA Division during the latter half of 1968, the need for helicopters grew. *"I was very fortunate in this,"* Davis was later to state, *"that the later model of the CH-46 (Boeing Vertol "Sea Knight") was arriving in-country in large numbers."*[28] The Super D model '46, featuring more powerful engines and redesigned rotor blades, significantly improved lift capabilities over the earlier 'A' models and could move more troops into battle faster.

In addition, due to his close working relationship with Army Lieutenant General Richard G. Stilwell, who commanded XXIV Corps which controlled Army and some Marine units in I Corps, Davis had the promise of Army helicopter support if needed. More important, however, was the creation of Provisional Marine Aircraft Group (MAG) 39 just north of Quang Tri city, and the subsequent assignment of a Marine air commander for northern I Corps who, as General Davis stated, *"had enough authority delegated to him … where he could execute things. He could order air units to do things."* [29]

Davis' concept of mobile operations depended not only on the helicopter, but on the extensive exploitation of intelligence gathered by small reconnaissance patrols, which he continuously employed throughout the division's area of responsibility. Operating within range of friendly artillery were the heavily armed "Stingray" patrols, whose mission was to find, fix, and destroy the enemy with all available supporting arms, and rapid reinforcement, if necessary. In the more remote areas, beyond artillery range, Davis used "Key Hole" patrols. Much smaller in size and armed with only essential small arms and ammunition, the function of these patrols was to observe. The 3rd Marine Division, Davis noted, *"never launched an operation without acquiring clear definition of the targets and objectives through intelligence confirmed by recon patrols. High mobility operations [were] too difficult and complex to come up empty or in disaster."* [30]

The collection of intelligence relative to the A Shau Valley and Base Area 611 preceded Operation Dewey Canyon by several months. Reconnaissance patrols found numerous signs of the NVA using the area extensively going back to the previous summer. On one such mission a 3rd Force Recon team found well-constructed stairways—making it easier for the NVA to traverse steep mountain trails hidden underneath triple-canopy foliage—and ran straight into a large communist force.

As former Recon Mike Green recalls in his personal memoir: *"Because of the danger of this mission, we had nine men instead of the usual eight. We also packed more "noise makers" than usual: 700 or 800 rounds and eight grenades instead of the usual 500 bullets and four grenades. Between our weapons, ammo, food, water, and other gear, we each carried about 100 pounds on our backs.*

"The order of march was James "Smitty" Smith (point), Wayne Thompson (slack or second point), Steve Laktash (patrol leader), George Boks (radio), John Romero (heavy weapons), Jerry Beasley, Dale "Doc" Watchorn (Corpsman), Randy Rhodes (secondary radio), and Mike Green (tail-end Charley and assistant patrol leader).

"We moved slowly up a finger that extended down from the mountains. The jungle was quiet and the team moved silently. Within 100 meters we found a small trail with several small, earthen ovens used for cooking. The faint aroma of wood fires lingered in the air. Several dry spots on the ground replaced the dew from the previous night and Doc decided they were not friendly dry spots. We continued up the finger another 200 to 300 meters and found a six-foot wide, hard-packed trail with log-reinforced steps and fighting trenches on each side. The trail was fairly straight and vegetation had been removed to about eight feet above the trail. The normal NVA trail was less than a foot wide and wandered around any rock or bush. This was a heavily used route. Alongside the trail were several wooden ammunition boxes, freshly made of what looked like pine, with Chinese lettering on the sides. Steve and I copied the lettering into our notebooks while the rest of team provided security. Doc and Smitty, who had crossed the trail, signaled they had spotted three NVA moving down the finger toward us. George was trying to contact Blue Plate (recon headquarters) on the radio but the high mountains and dense jungle precluded communication. Since we were in a deep valley and George could only whisper, Blue Plate could not hear him.

VICTORY BETRAYED — Ronald Winter

"Steve wanted to elude the NVA and circle back to the trail to look for additional signs of NVA activity. We immediately began retreating down the slope with George trying to raise Blue Plate. We moved about 100 meters to a spot where we'd had communication earlier. Steve turned us sideways across the finger while we stopped, to allow George to contact Blue Plate to advise them of the trail and sightings, and that the NVA were probably hunting us.

"Doc became trapped in wait-a-minute vines. These were less than the thickness of a pencil but very strong. Their larger cousins are what Tarzan uses to swing through the trees. They get their name from entangling feet and packs, and a Marine has to wait a minute to extract himself or cut the vines. Doc was suspended nearly upside down, trying to cut himself free.

"The area had dense undergrowth and visibility was only five to 15 feet. Randy and I were on the right flank with a small bush between us. We were all facing uphill toward the NVA when I spotted a pair of boots moving under a bush, no more than 10 feet from me. The selector switch on our M-16 rifles was under the right thumb and had three settings: Safe, Single Fire, and Automatic Fire. We always kept our weapons on safe since an accidental discharge would, at best, alert the enemy we were in the area or, at worst, shoot a teammate. I pushed the selector switch but nothing happened. My rifle had been brand new in January and I had fired several hundred rounds since then. But I had only moved the selector switch a few dozen times. It was not yet broken-in and was stuck. I moved my left hand to the switch, got a firm grip, and turned it to fully automatic. In that one second, the NVA moved around the bush and spotted Randy and me. We fired at the same time. I emptied half a magazine into the soldier and sprayed the area in front of me, then inserted a full magazine and blindly sprayed the brush. Just as I reached for the third magazine, I noticed the bush between Randy and me was ripped apart by bullets.

"As soon as I pulled the trigger, seven other members of Marblechamp began to fire, each sending out two magazines of automatic fire before switching to single fire. John carried the M-79 grenade launcher but was unable to fire because of the dense vegetation. At the same time the patrol of NVA, estimated at 20 *to 40 men, opened up with rifles and at least one light machine gun.*

"Steve was prone and had fired two magazines. He'd rolled on his side to extract another magazine from his cartridge belt when he noticed a small hole in the canopy above us. He told John to start lobbing M-79 rounds through the hole and not to miss the hole, since any grenades hitting foliage above us would spray shrapnel on top of us. The M-79 is a single shot weapon that breaks like a double-barrel shotgun for loading. Called a Blooper for the sound it makes when firing, its 40-millimeter, high explosive round is deadly. John was a master with the Blooper and could fire rapidly and accurately.

"The noise level was intense with 30 or 40 automatic and semi-automatic weapons firing from 10 or 15 feet away. The addition of at least one NVA machine gun, and the steady blast of Blooper rounds, added to the din.

"I rolled backward and landed on my pack but was suspended a foot or two in the air by a network of wait-a-minute vines. I struggled for a minute before pulling my Ka-Bar (fighting knife) from my pack strap to cut the vines. While I was doing that, the NVA were still firing. Luckily, we were down slope from them and they were shooting a foot or two above our heads. I still have visions of leaf litter falling on my face from the bullet-riddled vegetation above me.

"George had the radio handset keyed trying to raise Blue Plate when the firing started, and there's nothing like a firefight to get the attention of anyone listening on the radio. Blue Plate immediately confirmed that Marblechamp was in trouble and called the air base in Da Nang to scramble the jets. The helicopter crews were relaxing in their choppers on the landing pad at Vandegrift with a radio tuned to our frequency. They jumped into positions, started their helicopters, and were able to lift off in about two minutes. George requested an emergency extraction.

"Between the team's fire and John's grenades, the NVA broke contact. We again started down the hill but realized George was not with us. He was tangled in wait-a-minute vines. Steve and John returned for George and cut him loose from the vines. We headed down the hill at a pretty fast clip with Smitty and Wayne leap-frogging and conducting "recon-by-fire" in front of us while I fired

along our back trail to slow the NVA.

"*When we broke into the clearing, Steve was worried about where the NVA would appear and he led the team across the stream to avoid being flanked. We were taking machine gun fire and water was dancing in the stream from the impacts. John tripped in the stream and fell, losing the remainder of the M-79 rounds and was not able to locate them in the deep water. Wayne ran across the stream and stepped in a hole that was deeper than he was tall. He continued running until he surfaced on the other side of the hole.*

"*Blue Plate wanted Marblechamp to break contact and continue the mission. As commander on the ground, Steve wanted the extraction since the mission was compromised and he knew we were surrounded by a large enemy force. It would be nearly impossible for us to remain hidden. The chopper pilot argued with Blue Plate that this might be the only opportunity to pull us out. The pilot announced he was in-bound and Steve signaled with a smoke grenade. One chopper came in to pick us up while the crewmen fired machine guns over our heads into the tree line. As soon as we were aboard, the chopper lifted off and I dropped a smoke grenade into the tree line. We knocked out the Plexiglas windows on one side of the chopper and fired into the tree line as we lifted off. We moved across the river and orbited for a few minutes while the jets dropped bombs and fired rockets. We thanked the jet pilots for the quick response and the helicopters returned the team to Dong Ha. The team made sure we thanked the helicopter crews for being there to pull us out. The crew chief told us they had just replaced the windows.*" [31]

By late 1968, within the central portion of Quang Tri Province, communist units—including three battalions of the hardcore 812th Regiment that had launched massive but costly attacks against Marine units in the DMZ in 1967—had retreated into jungle sanctuaries on the Quang Tri-Thua Thien provincial border to resupply and reinforce. These units were nearly annihilated during the January 1968 Tet and post-Tet offensives after a disastrous attempt to overrun the provincial capital at Quang Tri City. In addition, their forward base areas and cache sites were destroyed by Marine and ARVN search-and-clear operations during the late summer and fall campaigns. By the end of 1968, an estimated 100,000 communist troops had been killed in I Corps alone,[32] 40,000 in northern I Corps, which helped reduce enemy strength.

Even so, enemy strength at the end of January 1969, within the Demilitarized Zone and Quang Tri Province, was estimated at 36,800, approximately 2,500 more than the December 1968 total. Of these, more than half were confirmed to be combat troops.[33]

In Thua Thien Province, directly south of Quang Tri, the enemy situation was similar. North Vietnamese Army units, with the exception of small forward elements of the combat hardened 4th and 5th Regiments, had withdrawn into the A Shau Valley and Laos under constant US and ARVN pressure during the previous year. These forward elements did launch occasional attacks by fire, but were forced to confine much of their effort to rice gathering and survival in the foothills of the province. Viet Cong local force units, such as they were after their devastating losses in the 1968 Tet Offensive, and the Viet Cong infrastructure, remained under steady pressure from Army, ARVN, and provincial forces, and likewise devoted much of their energy toward avoiding discovery. Nonetheless, the end-of-January estimates placed enemy strength within the province at 15,200, a 25-percent increase over December figures. To the west, in the A Shau Valley and beyond, there also were signs of increasing enemy activity. Roadwork was being conducted on Route 548 in the valley and on Route 922 in Laos. Vehicular traffic and troop movement was light at the beginning of the month, but picked up as January progressed, particularly in and around Route 922 and enemy Base Area 611 in Laos. General Davis, in commenting on the use of the Ho Chi Minh Trail, and the directives against US forces taking control of it, said, *"It makes me sick to sit on this hill and watch those 1,000 trucks go down those roads in Laos, hauling ammunition down south to kill Americans ...* "[34]

Although contact with communist forces was light in January, the free-world forces were not deceived. The communists had made the launching of spring-time offensives nearly a tradition, and after the country-wide communist assault in Tet 1968, American and South Vietnamese were not about to let their guard down. While the enemy generally avoided contact in January, American and South Vietnamese forces in northern I Corps continued their efforts at keeping him off balance, striking at his traditional base areas and infiltration routes, and increasing security within populated areas.[35]

AUTHOR'S OBSERVATIONS

In the Beginning

I served in HMM-161 starting at the Marine Corps Air Station, New River, North Carolina from 1966 when the squadron's colors were returned to the states after its first Vietnam tour in 1965-1966. I stayed with the squadron for more than two years, including seven months during its second Vietnam tour that lasted from 1968 to 1970. (I spent the rest of my Vietnam tour with HMM-164.)

HMM-161 flew the Sikorsky UH-34 helicopter in its first tour but transitioned to the Boeing Vertol CH-46 models prior to the second tour. While in New River, during 1967 and early 1968, the squadron rebuilt, trained technicians and pilots, and prepared to return to war. On April 20, 1968, HMM-161, consisting of 24 D Model 46s, departed New River in flights of four, en route to the Marine Corps Air Base, El Toro, California – the first leg of its journey to Vietnam.

By this time I was a skilled avionics technician. I also flew on test flights and qualified as an aerial gunner on the Browning M-2, .50 caliber machine gun. I made the flight as part of the crew of Yankee Romeo (HMM-161's tail designation) 39. Three flight days later the entire squadron appeared in the skies over southern California and spelled out 161 in the air before landing.

HMM-161 flew over the southeastern United States' woodlands and farms, saw the Mississippi River from above, passed over the oil fields of Texas, the Great American Desert, and the lower reaches of the Rocky Mountains before stunning the populace below with the thunder of 24 war birds passing overhead.

The squadron then boarded the USS Princeton, LPH-5, for the journey across the Pacific Ocean and the South China Sea to Vietnam. During the ocean voyage we weathered a typhoon, and squadron Commanding Officer Lt. Col. Paul W. Niesen landed a '46 in the ocean to rescue a sailor who fell overboard. The squadron arrived in Quang Tri, South Vietnam on May 17, 1968 and began flying combat missions the next day. I consider the time I spent in HMM-161—especially on the journey from New River to Quang Tri–to be one of the greatest adventures of my life. I flew more than 300 missions as an aerial gunner, and I still stay in contact with my fellow Marines through periodic reunions.

AUTHOR'S OBSERVATIONS

Strong? Point Obstacle System

Robert McNamara's Strong Point Obstacle System, or the McNamara Line as it was universally known, was viewed with disdain and derision by the Marines who had to build it, protect their own forces at the same time, and live with the daily reminder – in incoming artillery – that it didn't and never could work.

In July 1967, Marines launching Operation Buffalo were caught in an artillery and automatic weapons crossfire, specifically because they were tasked with two full-time missions, build the McNamara line and maintain security simultaneously. Neither task could be completed to satisfaction if Marines were continually siphoned away from their primary tasks to attend to other requirements imposed by bureaucrats thousands of miles away. As a direct result of the political and bureaucratic interference, a half-company, nearly 100 Marines were killed in the opening salvos of the Operation, some even by NVA soldiers wielding flame throwers that were used on the Marines as they advanced through a chokepoint.

In the long run Operation Buffalo was successful, but the loss of so many Marines simply due to bureaucratic interference with their tactics is unconscionable.

Many Marines saw the McNamara line as a prime example of "rich kids playing at war," and costing the lives of American troops, while the politicians and bureaucrats sat back in *"the World,"* sipping bourbon – or whatever their favorite beverage may have been – and shrugging off their mistakes as good ideas that were *'poorly executed.'*

41

INITIAL ASSAULT

"Marines were heard to talk about the good old days back on Shiloh."

Operation Dewey Canyon initially was an extension of Operation Dawson River which began in late 1968 and covered areas of Quang Tri Province north and west of Khe Sanh. Enemy contact during Dawson River was comparatively light, and the decision to move into the A Shau and Da Krong valleys is generally considered to have taken place over the course of a few days in mid-January.[36] But the preparations that made Dewey Canyon possible actually occurred months earlier. Col. (ret.) Warren Wiedhahn, then a major, was the S-4 (logistics) officer for the 3rd Battalion, 9th Marines from August to December 1968, and remembers, *We plotted and planned Dewey Canyon in November and December. Dewey Canyon was a different operation than those that preceded it, in that it was 100 percent supported by air,"* he noted.[37] The planning initially included coordination with the Army's 101st Airborne Division,[38] but deployment of that unit on the operation did not materialize, and included a backup force from the 3rd Marines if more manpower became necessary. That proved to be a fortuitous piece of planning as later events would prove.

The first stage of the movement into the Area of Operations was to open three previously established fire support bases which stretched southward from Vandegrift. On 18 January units of Lieutenant Colonel Elliott R. Laine, Jr.'s 3rd Battalion, 9th Marines re-secured FSB Henderson, eight kilometers southwest of Ca Lu, in conjunction with a brief operation in the Ba Long Valley. This operation was a natural corollary to the base security mission picked

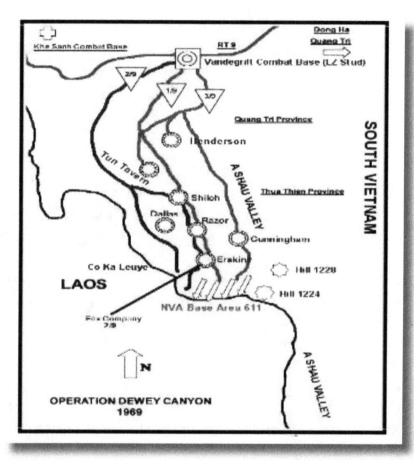

Figure 8 Layout of Operation Dewey Canyon Jan.-March 1969

up by the 9th Marines as it returned to Vandegrift from Dawson River West. On 20 January, Company L, 3rd Battalion, 9th Marines reopened FSB Tun Tavern, unoccupied since early December 1968, after a team from the 3rd Reconnaissance Battalion checked for mines and booby traps. Battery D, 2nd Battalion, 12th Marines occupied reconstructed artillery positions later the same day, and began shelling the previously occupied, but currently empty of friendly troops FSB Shiloh, another eight kilometers south. On 21 January, shortly after Marine air prepped Shiloh, Company A, 1st Battalion, 9th Marines occupied the fire base. Insertion of the artillery was delayed due to a fuse malfunction on one 750-pound bomb that detonated on impact instead of above ground, wiping out two previously constructed 105mm howitzer parapets, half of a third, and two ammunition berms. To repair the damage required seven hours of bulldozer work.[39]

With the reoccupation of Shiloh by two batteries of the 12th Marines, a forward Logistics Staging Area (LSA) was established on the site and stocked with 5,000 rounds of artillery ammunition, and a 10-day supply of rations and batteries for an infantry battalion. As it turned out, Marines of Company A—who were assigned the mission of providing security for the two artillery batteries on Shiloh in those early days—considered duty there to be a *"vacation"* compared to what they would face in the very near future. In addition to the normal patrols, as Colonel (Ret.) Wesley L. Fox, then a first lieutenant and company commander, later remembered, *"A platoon a day went off the hill to the small river at the foot ... for swimming and fishing. Swimming and lying in the sun on the nice sand bar were great, but the real treat was the fish provided by the fishing expedition. The platoons would wind up their day at the river by throwing grenades in the deep holes and simply wading out and picking up the fish that floated to the top."* In the remaining months of the battle, with the company engaged in fierce firefights, while experiencing shortages of both water and rations, and exhaustive patrols, Fox continued, *"Marines were heard to talk about the good old days back on Shiloh."* With Henderson, Tun Tavern, and Shiloh reoccupied, the 9th Marines were now poised to launch attacks into the new area of operations.[40]

On the morning of 22 January, four companies of Lieutenant

VICTORY BETRAYED — Ronald Winter

Colonel George C. Fox's 2nd Battalion lifted off from Vandegrift with a two-fold mission: Companies E and H were to assault a 600-meter hilltop about eight kilometers south-southeast of Shiloh, while Companies F and G would secure a landing zone, Dallas, five kilometers beyond to the southwest. Except for scattered small arms fire the landings of Companies E and H went unopposed, and work on the fire support base, named Razor, began immediately. The first fire support base established in the Area of Operations was named by Colonel Barrow in honor of General Davis. "Razor" was the nickname given Davis by Major General James M. Master, Sr., when both served on Okinawa in the early 60s: *The razor cuts to the root of problems.*[41]

Razor was like other bases constructed by the 9th Marines' infantry, artillery, and engineer team during the previous eight months of mountain warfare, but technically more difficult. Trees measuring three to four feet in diameter—the largest encountered—had to be cleared, a job which posed major problems for the inexperienced Marines of Company H. According to Captain David F. Winecoff, commanding officer of the company: *We went in with … enough power saws and axes to do the job—if we had the experienced people to work these things. But, I found out that there are very few people in Hotel Company, and we were the ax swingers, that knew how to swing an ax properly, and we immediately proceeded to bust about 50 to 60 percent of our axes. It was only through the cooperation of the engineers and all hands concerned in Hotel Company [that] with the power saws and the limited amount of axes that we got … Fire Support Base Razor opened up in time … It was quite a feat.* Winecoff's Marines cleared the trees, but the gentle slope on one side, coupled with two mounds on the flanks, required the use of light bulldozers that were brought in by helicopter to widen the landing zone, and build gun pits and ammunition berms.[42]

VICTORY BETRAYED — Ronald Winter

Among the air crews who delivered the first troops and equipment, including artillerymen and engineers as well as infantry, to open Razor, was Master Gunnery Sergeant. (ret.) Jack Payne, who was then a Master Sergeant. He, and the pilots and crews of heavy helicopter squadron HMH-463, were tasked with moving a mountain of equipment and supplies to the initial outposts in Operation Dewey Canyon. Payne arrived at Provisional MAG 39 in Quang Tri the previous May with medium helicopter squadron HMM-161, which offloaded from the helicopter carrier USS Princeton (LPH 5) on 17 May, 1968 with 24 CH-46 Super D helicopters. There they joined HMM-262 which flew the CH-46 D models, and VMO-6 which consisted essentially of Bell UH-1 "Huey" gunships and small observation aircraft. Although he was tasked with higher level CH-46 maintenance control duties when he first arrived in Quang Tri, Payne, a gunnery sergeant at the time, was a factory-trained CH-53 specialist, and soon was reassigned to HMH-463 at Marble Mountain, just outside the Da Nang Airbase. Payne recalled that the CH-53A models were having serious maintenance problems that were exacerbated by supply chain problems, and they needed experienced and trained help, immediately. He spent six months in the southern base and was promoted to Master Sergeant before being reassigned as NCO in charge (NCOIC) of an 8-helicopter CH-53 detachment that was based back in Quang Tri. The reassignment was perfectly timed as far as Dewey Canyon's needs were concerned, giving the CH-53 pilots and crews a full month to become acquainted with air operations in northernmost I Corps. It was this detachment that was primarily responsible for moving not only artillery pieces, but the equipment and materiel that was needed for construction of a proper Fire Support Base, including chain saws, explosives, primer cord—that could be wrapped around trees and detonated to blow them down—and even small bulldozers. Later in the operation Payne remembers loads of giant timbers being flown to the A Shau Valley to reinforce gun pits and bunkers. And, as with most others who participated in Dewey Canyon, Payne, who also flew as a .50 caliber machine gunner, remembers clouds, lots of clouds and rain. *"There were times,"* he said, *"when we had to be vectored in, (by radar) because we couldn't see anything due to the monsoon rains."* [43]

But heavy lift capabilities weren't the only missions for the CH-53s. Although not used in Dewey Canyon, where their primary missions were resupply or heavy lift missions, Payne said, *"The 53s could be used as a combat weapon, taking 20, 50-gallon drums of napalm out and dropping them on targets. We had an X on the cockpit bubble for aiming."* Since his squadron's official designation was HMH-463, *"We (informally) called ourselves the 463rd Loose Wing Bomber Squadron,"* Payne recalled.

In the rapid buildup that followed the opening of Razor, CH-46 helicopters, under the control of the wing Direct Air Support Center (DASC) and the protective umbrella of gunships and observation aircraft, brought 1,544 Marines and 46 tons of cargo into the landing zone. By the evening of 23 January, a battery of 105mm howitzers was in place. The following day, the regimental command group moved to Razor and occupied the gently sloping finger on the fire base's northwestern edge. The 2nd Battalion, 12th Marines' command and fire control groups followed a short time later. Control of the Fire Direction Center (FDC) and Fire Support Coordination Center (FSCC) was then passed from Vandegrift to Razor without loss of continuity or centralized fire control. Six days after the introduction of Laine's 3rd Battalion, the regiment was well into the zone of action. [44]

On the morning of 25 January 1969, after heavy air strikes, Laine's battalion assaulted three landing zones atop Ca Ka Va, a 1,100-meter-long razorback ridgeline, 6,000 meters south-southwest of FSB Razor. A short time later an artillery advance party and a team of engineers heli-lifted into the landing zones and began construction of what was to become FSB Cunningham, named for the first Marine aviator, Lieutenant Alfred A. Cunningham. The first wave of helicopters that brought troops into the zone was led by Lt. Col. (ret.) James Loop, then a major with HMM-161. Loop said he had attended a briefing session at the 9th Marines headquarters near Vandegrift the previous day and then, accompanied by a gunship pilot from VMO-6, reconnoitered the area to scout possible landing zones. *"We had excellent weather that day and the day of the initial assault,"* Loop recalled. But 24 hours—and plenty of artillery and air strikes—brought significant changes to the area. One day earlier he had seen verdant jungle and hilltops. But as he led the first flight of helicopters into the zone, Loop later said, *"It was nothing but a bald hilltop with a bunch of smoking stumps."* The air and artillery had done their work, but the zone was still just a rough spot in what had been an impenetrable jungle.[45] *"We did the best we could to drop the troops on any spot we could find,"* recalled Col. (ret.) Joseph Snyder, then a first lieutenant flying with HMM-161. Despite the irregularity of the zone the troop lift went smoothly, and the success of the initial assault was played out several times in the coming days as the operation proceeded.[46]

From an artillery standpoint, Cunningham was ideal. Being at the center of the planned operational area and large enough to accommodate an integrated battalion position, it represented a simple solution to fire support requirements and coordination. As for the 9th Marines, its 11-kilometer artillery fan extended south and southwest almost to the limit of the area of operations. Within the next four days the regimental command group and five artillery batteries—consisting of 6 artillery pieces each—moved into position

49

on Cunningham. Mortar and D Batteries, the former from Vandegrift and the latter from Tun Tavern, were in place by sunset on 25 January. The 1st and 3rd Provisional 155mm Howitzer Batteries—the largest artillery pieces to be permanently part of Operation Dewey Canyon—were heli-lifted in by Army CH-47 Chinooks and CH-54 Skycranes on 28 January from Ca Lu and Shiloh, respectively. When E Battery moved from Shiloh to Cunningham the following day, the artillery movement into the Da Krong Valley was complete.[47] Despite the fast pace of the movement into the Area of Operation, the amount of work that went into preparing each Fire Support Base was not reduced. Creating a gun position was not simply a matter of providing a flat space for the placement of artillery pieces. A defensive berm made of earth surrounded each gun while dirt-filled ammo containers and sandbags helped fortify the position. The gun platform required a hole in the platform to accommodate the recoil when high-angle firing was called for, which was quite often in Dewey Canyon due to the mountainous terrain. In addition, grids had to be established to ensure that the artillery rounds were fired to the correct position, aiming stakes placed, and defenses prepared. In a relatively short time the amount of work required was completed and the operation was ready to proceed.[48]

The pace of helicopter operations turned to *"normal resupply,"* Loop said, *"mostly bullets and beans."* Despite the pace and due to the deteriorating weather, however, *"Sometimes we got through and sometimes we had to come back and return the load."* Also, as the operation progressed, *"There were a lot of medevacs,"* Loop said.

Although the weather played a major factor in how much infantry, and by extension, artillery activity occurred on a given day, there still was ongoing activity at the fire bases even when they were socked in by the weather. LCpl. Alan Sargent, who was assigned to

VICTORY BETRAYED — Ronald Winter

Fire Direction Control, remembers, *"We shared working party chores, (with other Marines in the battery) which generally consisted of humping ammo from wherever the helicopters dropped them to the individual gun pits, which each had an ammo bunker."* Ammo bunkers were small and made from the empty ammo boxes after the 2 rounds in each were removed. The boxes were then filled with dirt and stacked up to build the walls. Portable steel plating (PSP) was used as roofing, and sandbags were stacked on top to hold down the PSP and provide blast protection. *"Filling and stacking sandbags was a monumental chore, and we did a lot of it,"* Sargent said. *"Additionally, we built an Exec Pit (executive officer's pit) where the (battery) XO, and recorder worked, and usually lived."* As Col. (retired) Harvey Barnum, then a captain and E Battery Commanding Officer, explained, *"From there the executive officer could see all the guns, and they could see him. He was linked to the guns by telephone, but they could also use hand and arm signals to communicate. The exec pit controlled the firing."* It contained a land line to FDC, and various radios for communicating with HQ and FO's (forward observers), and land lines to each gun to pass on firing data and control the actual firing. *"Normally, each gun built their own bunkers,"* Sargent said. *"FDC built theirs, and the recorder built the exec pit—with help. FDC required a bunker too. We needed to protect the maps, radios, worksheets required to calculate the firing data, and cover at night because we needed light to work."* Once the work for the battery was complete, there still was more to do. *"Personnel bunkers were almost always built, too. These were used for sleeping, cooking, resting, etc. On a few occasions, when in the rear or at an LZ that wasn't built up, and where we weren't going to stay long, we used tents."*

Once the battery was completed, the fire missions began. Sargent explained that, *"FDC consisted of about 8 Marines—a section chief, assistant section chief and 6 or so others. We were usually on a 12-hour shift, with one Marine operating the radio and communicating with an FO*

(Forward Observer) or battalion HQ, depending on who was controlling the fire mission, and communicating with the exec pit via land line, alerting them to pending fire missions and passing the gun data to the recorder in the exec pit after it was calculated. There was also a Marine plotting the targets on the map and the shift was supervised by either the section chief or assistant, depending on who had the responsibility for that shift. The supervisor also double-checked any firing data worked up by the person on the sticks—which is what we called the slide rules—used to calculate firing data. It was usually a lot more informal than this, because we only occasionally had a full crew."

Starting with a call from battalion headquarters or a forward observer, the normal sequence of events as listed by Sargent was:

1. An FO or Battalion HQ radios in and alerts FDC to a fire mission.

2. FDC calls the exec pit and alerts them.

3. The FO gives FDC the map coordinates and requests ammunition type: WP (white phosphorus), HE (high explosive), smoke, firecracker or beehive, and specifies whether to fire an air burst or impact, which determines the type of fuse to affix to the rounds.

4. FDC passes along the type of round and fuses needed to the exec pit.

5. The map coordinates are given to the map guy to plot, he then gives us back the deflection and distance to target.

6. FDC passes the quadrant (rough deflection) on to the exec pit to allow them to point the guns in the approximate direction.

7. Based upon the distance and direction, FDC, using the slide rules calculates the deflection, elevation, and

number of powder bags required. If an air burst is needed, we calculate the flight time for the rounds, to set timed fuses, and we determine if high angle firing is required, which was almost all the time because I Corps was so hilly.

8. FDC passes this info along to the exec pit with the number of registration rounds required. The FO usually needed to walk the rounds to the target because of the rough estimate of target location. They usually did this with only 1 or 2 guns.

9. The exec pit told us when the battery was ready to fire.

10. We told the FO we were ready and waited for his signal to fire.

11. We pass the fire command to the exec pit.

12. We notify the FO of the shot.

13. The FO usually called for an adjustment after the rounds hit, normally something like, *"Left 50 (meters), or long 50."*

14. The adjustment was made on the map and the firing data recalculated. (The adjustment directions are relative to the view of the FO, not the battery, so, when he called for an adjustment we adjusted the target on the map appropriately. Left 50 from his point of view may mean FDC has to add 50 meters to the distance to the target from the firing point of view.)

15. The new elevation and deflection are passed to the exec pit.

16. This process continues until the rounds are striking

where the FO wants them.

17. At this point we usually fired the entire battery for the number of rounds requested.

On the other end of the mission, the Forward Observer was waiting to see the impacts to determine where to send the next rounds. Col. Barnum recalled that based on whether the firing mission was a priority, it could take up to a couple of minutes before the first rounds impacted. 2nd Lt. Jay Standish—a Forward Observer from the 2nd Battalion, 12th Marines who was assigned to the 2nd Battalion, 9th Marines—also recalled a mission he called in on a follow-up operation after Dewey Canyon, where a reinforced Marine platoon was boxed in by a regimental-sized NVA force and was taking horrendous incoming. Standish called in the mission *"Danger close,"* which meant closer than 100 yards to the friendly forces. The first two rounds hit within 90 seconds he recalled and were exactly on target. The remainder of the mission decimated the NVA force.

But even after the missions were complete, the work didn't stop. *"When shells were fired, the canisters were just thrown over the hill, way too many to recycle I guess,"* Sargent recalled. *"Unused powder bags were usually burned to keep them from piling up and creating a hazard. We did have the occasional problem with powder bags that somehow got thrown over the hill and caught fire. There was usually some unused ammunition over the side of the hill too (I don't recall how it got there), and we had several fires that would 'cook off' those rounds. That was disturbing, to say the least. When not on duty, work parties or guard duty used up a lot of time."* Work parties were either the ammo humping, or what in some venues was termed *"honey bucket"* burning duty, which involved removing 55-gallon drums that were cut in half and placed below the seats in the heads, or outhouses. *"Each day, when possible, the Corpsman would need to take the 1/2 barrels and mix them with diesel fuel and burn them. We provided the disgusting manual labor.*" Guard duty was an ever-present occupation whereby the artillerymen and other Marines joined the infantry for perimeter duty. Guard duty was nowhere near as popular an occupation as the continuous search for a way to make C-rations edible. *"Some people seemed to be able to do it,"* Sargent said. *"I just ate chicken and noodles for a whole year. I couldn't handle the other crap no matter how hungry I got. I supplemented the chicken and noodles with pound cake, crackers and peanut butter or jam, trop bars, and cigarettes. I smoked almost continuously. I guess it helped kill the hunger pangs. I probably shouldn't be alive, just based upon how much I smoked in that one year."* [49]

Soon after Cunningham opened, a small regimental forward logistical support area, capable of daily resupplying eight rifle companies with rations, water, batteries, and small arms ammunition, was established. A tactical logistical group (Tac Log), used primarily in amphibious operations, also was created, enabling the supply officer to work closely with the regimental commander, the operations officer, and the air liaison officer. As Major Charles G. Bryan, the regimental S-4, (Logistics Officer) noted: *"The procedure permitted the establishment of realistic priorities to minimize interference with tactical operations and also to ensure maximum utilization of available helicopter assets. And it further provided for a more effective control and coordination of resupply operations."* The tactical logistical group was set up *"with an administrative Tac Log net from each battalion, with the logistics requirements being passed through the regime. The regiment would then pass these logistic requirements to the personnel in the rear at Vandegrift who would ensure that these supplies were promptly staged on the LSA and lifted to the field."* This technique would prove invaluable as the regiment moved into the second phase of the operation, now called Dewey Canyon. After a majority of the regiment was deployed, and the area of operations expanded, the operational codename was changed from Dawson River South to

Dewey Canyon. However, Dawson River South remained in effect for those elements of the 9th Marines still at Fire Support Bases Tun Tavern and Henderson.[50]

AUTHOR'S OBSERVATIONS

Lance Coolies

The rank Lance Corporal is number three on the enlisted ladder, one rank above Private First Class and two above Private.

Many Marines consider Lance Corporals to be the backbone of the corps. While they have more responsibility than privates or PFCs, such as fire team leaders in infantry units, they haven't reached the level of responsibility entrusted to corporals.

Corporals are the first rank to hold the distinction of Non-Commissioned Officers and as such are responsible not only for their own actions, but for those of lower-ranking Marines assigned to their area of responsibility.

Thus Lance Corporals often are assigned many of the arduous tasks required of units both in the field and back at fixed bases. These duties can range from ammo bearers to guard duty, mess duty in the rear, or the always detested *"honey bucket"* details.

Quite often those who hold the rank of Lance Corporal take a perverse sense of pride in their status, especially when promotion to the rank of corporal escapes them. Some even referred to themselves as 'Lance Coolies' to reflect the burdensome chores which they perform. The longer a person stayed in that rank, the higher their status on a somewhat inverse scale.

I was meritoriously promoted to PFC in boot camp, and I was promoted to Lance Corporal nine months later, three months after arriving at HMM-161. But I stayed in that rank for the next 27 months–longer than many Marines spent on active duty. After transferring to HMM-164 I was quickly promoted to Corporal.

Go Figure!

MOVING ON OUT

"They knew our routes and were ready for us.
We had contact almost every day."

Following the rapid movement of the regiment into the area of operations, companies of the 2nd and 3rd Battalions moved out from Razor and Cunningham on 24 and 25 January, initiating Phase II. Their mission was to clear the area around the two fire support bases, secure the flanks, and then gradually move into position along the Da Krong's east-west axis, designated Phase Line Red, for Phase III. This placed the 3rd Battalion on the eastern flank and the 2nd Battalion on the western flank near the Laotian border. The 1st Battalion, 9th Marines, under Lieutenant Colonel George W. Smith, would take the middle once the two battalions were in place. Second phase objectives included: seizing the Co Ka Leuye ridge line, assigned to Company G, construction of FSB Erskine, four kilometers southwest of Cunningham, by Company F, and occupation of LZ Lightning and Tornado, four kilometers northeast of Cunningham, by Company K.[51]

Patrolling 2,000 to 3,000 meters apart, the two battalions encountered screening forces of major enemy units thought to be operating further south. The Marines were fighting elements of the NVA 5th and 6th regiments, the 65th Artillery Regiment, and the 83rd Engineer Regiment.[52] Engagements with single NVA soldiers or small bands of support troops were commonplace, and the ensuing firefights short but deadly. Lt. Miles Davis, a platoon commander and later executive officer with Company K remembered that, *"The*

VICTORY BETRAYED — Ronald Winter

NVA defended in small 'killer' teams—three to four men and a machine gun." Their long-time familiarity with the A Shau and the routes back to Laos gave the NVA a distinct advantage over the assaulting Marines, Davis remembers. *"They knew our routes and were ready for us. We had contact almost every day."* Davis, who later was wounded and medevaced out of Dewey Canyon, related that there was no special treatment for him just because he was the general's son. Decades later Davis remarked that, *"I spent the whole time in the jungle."* If there was anything special about his participation in Dewey Canyon it was that General Davis would occasionally order his command helicopter to land at whatever landing zone was closest to his son's position to check in with him. But, when his presence served as a trigger to enemy gunners who would begin shelling the LZ, the general stopped *"dropping in."*[53]

On 25 January, one contact by Company M with a small enemy force led to the discovery of a sophisticated four-strand communications network. Running from Laos into Base Area 101 to the east, the line was strung between tree-mounted porcelain insulators and well concealed by overhead cover. A five-man special Marine and Army intelligence team tapped the wire and eventually broke the NVA code, but no information was provided to the 3rd Battalion as it was *"presumed to be of strategic rather than tactical value,"* noted Lieutenant Colonel Laine.

Another significant find during the first stage of Phase II was the 88th NVA Field Hospital discovered by Company F, 2nd Battalion, near the Song Da Krong, (Da Krong River). The complex consisted of eight large permanent buildings capable of accommodating 150 to 160 patients. A detailed search revealed large quantities of Russian-made stainless steel surgical instruments, antibiotics, foodstuffs, and evidence that the area had been evacuated the previous day. On the afternoon of 31 January, Company G, under Captain Daniel

VICTORY BETRAYED — Ronald Winter

A. Hitzelberger, launched its attack on Co Ka Leuye (Hill 1175) from LZ Dallas. After a short skirmish with a small group of NVA soldiers who sought to draw it into an ambush at sunset, the company crossed a tributary of the Da Krong and advanced 500 meters up the mountain before settling in for the night. The following morning the Marines continued their climb, roping up sheer rock cliffs and traversing slopes with grades averaging 65 to 75 degrees. As the day progressed, the weather began to deteriorate, adding yet another obstacle. Heavy rains alternated with drizzle and dense fog, reducing the hard, red Vietnamese soil to mud, visibility to 25 meters, and the ceiling to zero. Despite weather and terrain problems, Company G continued the climb toward the objective.

It was during this advance that the NVA revealed the desperation with which they faced the Marines, and the extremes they would go to when fighting in Operation Dewey Canyon. As recalled by then 2nd Lt. Jay Standish, the NVA tried out different tactics to confuse the Marines or stop their advance. Finding NVA soldiers strapped to trees where they fired on the advancing Marines with sniper rifles, or waiting until the Marines were below them and dropping grenades on them, was not unusual. In this case, however, as Company G Marines approached the base of Co Ka Leuye, the NVA took to firing at them from the trees armed not with standard weapons or even sniper rifles, but with crossbows, Standish said. Whether they were hoping to use secrecy as a weapon, since there would be no sounds from firing the crossbow bolts, or they were hoping to demoralize the Marines, the tactic didn't work. *"Fortunately, they weren't very good shots,"* Standish said, and the bolts didn't hit the intended targets.

During the climb up Co Ka Leuye, Cpl. Lewis Weber, a squad leader with Golf Company remembers, *"The going was tough due to the*

VICTORY BETRAYED — Ronald Winter

sharp incline, and there was no trail. Some of us tied our 10-foot long pieces of rope to one another so as not to fall backwards. At times, I had to crawl on my hands and knees to keep from falling. Reaching the summit of Hill 1175 was exhausting. The temperature atop the mountain was in the 40s or low 50s, and none of us was accustomed to being cold. The calves of my legs were cramping up bad from humping up the hill for the past four days. The pain was excruciating. Staff Sergeant (Donald) Burgess had each squad in the first platoon set up defensive positions, which were very close to one another due to the small area on the peak. There wasn't very much room to maneuver and all three platoons were cramped together. I set up two-hour watches with my three fire teams and the squad command post, so the guys could get some rest. Before this, however, I scrounged down the last bit of C rations I had, and some left over Long Rations. We referred to them as Long Rats, which was a new type of dry freeze, mostly used by the U. S. Army. A bag of Long Rats mixed with water was very tasty, especially when I was starving coming down the hill. I still preferred heating up the cans of C rations, but the bags were much lighter." The Marines settled in for what became a long, miserable night. They strained their eyes outward, trying to determine if movement in the fog was caused by enemy soldiers sneaking up on them, or merely breezes, parting then reconnecting the thick clouds. They listened intently, not sure if sounds coming from the jungle were caused by equipment and boot treads, or just the constant rain running off the thick foliage and slapping on the covering of the jungle floor. *"We were tired, hungry, and cold and someone got the bright idea to start a fire,"* Weber recalls. *"I do not know who gave the okay, but all of a sudden, campfires were popping up all over the place. (It was) pitch dark and foggy. I figured Lieutenant Langford gave permission after conferring with Captain Hitzelberger. No matter, I told the other fire teams it was okay. Normally it was a big taboo to have fires since the NVA would be able to spot our positions, but under the circumstances, I could not see more than 25 feet in front of me anyway."*

VICTORY BETRAYED — Ronald Winter

As Hitzelberger's company moved up Co Ka Leuye, the two other regimental objectives were taken. Company F secured the ground for FSB Erskine on 1 February, but was prevented from developing the position by the same bad weather hampering Company G's movement. Four kilometers east of Cunningham, Company K secured a landing zone and began construction of FSB Lightning. Within hours of completion, the 1st and 2nd Battalions, 2nd ARVN Regiment, plus the 1st Battalion, 62nd Artillery Regiment (ARVN) lifted into the fire support base just before inclement weather halted all helicopter operations. Predictably, enemy-initiated attacks increased during this period of bad weather. On 2 February, FSB Cunningham received 30 to 40 rounds from one or more enemy 122mm field guns located on or near the border.

Col. (ret.) John Wilkes, then a captain and CO of the 155mm towed-howitzer battery, remembers standing alongside one of the battery's guns and seeing an explosion down in the valley below the battery position. Briefly, *"We thought the grunts had come across a dud round,"* and destroyed it, Wilkes remembered. Then he got the sinking feeling that it might have been an aiming round from the communist guns and yelled for the gun crew to take cover.

Wilkes and the section chief sprinted for a nearby bunker, but a 122 shell hit about seven steps behind him, exploding a powder bunker and killing three members of the gun crew. The section chief, who had been in front of Wilkes, was wounded, but Wilkes was launched into the air, and while suffering massive bruising, miraculously was not hit by shrapnel.

A half-century later, *"I still think of losing three good men,"* Wilkes recalled.

The shell temporarily took out one of the battery's 155mm howitzers, melting the sight and burning off the tires. *"But we didn't need the tires, and we had a spare sight,"* so the gun was quickly back in action. Despite the incoming, the battalion's batteries maintained uninterrupted counter-battery fire at the unseen enemy. The 2nd Battalion, 12th Marines sustained a total of five killed and an equal number of wounded.

The sporadic attacks continued throughout the operation, and while some of the communist guns were in Laos just beyond the maximum range of the battalion's 155mm howitzers, Wilkes said they occasionally scored a hit on communist positions that were closer. The Army's 175mm guns, further to the rear, proved inaccurate at that distance, but were used to harass. Therefore, the only means of delivering effective counter-battery was by air. If the guns could be visually located, they could be destroyed. However, it soon became apparent that if an aerial observer (AO) remained on station for any length of time, all enemy fire would cease. Therefore, as Colonel Barrow later noted, *"counter-battery was a simple thing of always having an AO up."* The fire support base continued to receive enemy incoming throughout the operation at sporadic but frequent intervals, notably when the observers left the area, even for short periods.[54]

"Every time they shot it was just a couple of rounds at a time," Wilkes said. *"But every time they hit, I would go out, dig up the fuses, get reverse azimuths and trajectories,"* and use that data to plot return fire. *"Sometimes we'd hear secondary explosions,"* indicating a hit on the communist positions, he noted. However, it was still a matter of weeks before the infantry advanced close enough to the Laotian border, and additional firebases were opened that gave more accurate responses to communist salvos.[55]

By 3 February, after four days of bad weather, Colonel Barrow had to decide whether to hold present positions or pull back to more easily supported positions. He questioned whether the regiment had overextended itself by placing Company G on Co Ka Leuye. With no relief in sight, and helicopter resupply and medical evacuations halted throughout the area, Barrow instructed the 2nd and 3rd Battalions to pull in their companies and hold them close to areas they could easily support. The decision proved to be a wise one, since Razor and Cunningham were well-stocked with rations and small arms ammunition. Artillery ammunition, however, was in short supply. The 2nd Battalion, 12th Marines had attempted to stock extra shells, but the scarcity of heavy-lift helicopters (Marine CH-53s, and Army CH-47 Chinooks and CH-54 Skycranes), and the weather made it impossible to achieve the initial stockage objectives. Without the reserve, artillery missions had to be reduced.[56] The impact of the weather was noted in a letter Lt. John Cochenour, executive officer of Battery E wrote home. *"Fogged in again today! Seems like it's been like this forever. They did manage to get two helicopters in yesterday with some water and ammo—but more important we got a couple people out ... so the mail went out too. This weather has really held up our operation, and it's quite likely once we finally jump off that we may not come back in for TET as it was planned. We were supposed to go back in for TET (starts Feb. 17) as a reaction force in case they tried another offensive—but have my doubts that we will now. Things look too promising right here in the A Shau."*

For the first 10 days of February, the battalion fired 6,078 rounds, assisting only engaged units. Warren Wiedhahn, by then the Executive Officer of the 3rd Battalion, noted that the operation at this point, literally *"was stopped for 10 days due to logistics."*

With the operation fully dependent on air resupply there was no Plan B, since there were no roads, making motor vehicle resupply impossible. In addition, there were no navigable rivers into the Area of Operation. As noted previously, Col. Wiedhahn served as the 9th Marines' logistics officer from August to December 1968 and was involved in the planning stages of Dewey Canyon when it was still a germ of an idea, long before it had a name. *"Air insertion (of supplies and manpower) and extraction was the key,"* he said, thus it was helicopter resupply or nothing. Except for Company G, 2nd Battalion, all rifle companies took defensive positions, or were quickly moving into one by 4 February: Company L was on Cunningham, while I, K, and M companies were close by, Company H was on Razor, Company F was on Erskine, and Company E was at LZ Dallas.[57]

On the morning of 5 February, Capt. Hitzelberger's company began retracing its steps back down the summit of Hill 1175. Weber recalled that, *"I was looking forward to returning to LZ Dallas for some rest and especially food. I was starving like the rest of the guys. Our platoon moved out last as tail-end Charlie, guarding both flanks and the rear of our unit. The descent was a lot easier, but steep and slippery."* However, as Capt. Hitzelberger later reported, *"As we came down off of 1175, my point element, which was from the 3rd Platoon, observed three NVA off to the right. Because of the contacts we had the previous day, we decided to check out the area a little bit further. So, I held the column in place and allowed the point fire team to go out to see if there were any more forces there or take the three NVA if they could. Our point then came under fire."* Back at the rear of the column, Weber recalled that, *"Suddenly, I heard numerous loud explosions and automatic gunfire from down below. The pitch of the gunfire was distinctly from AK-47's, but I had no idea where the explosions came from. They were definitely not mortars or I would have heard the tubes popping. Although neither gunfire nor explosions were impacting near us, I knew the point platoon was catching hell. The word came back to watch the flanks for NVA. Next, I could hear men shouting frantically and machinegun fire."* From what Captain Hitzelberger was able to piece together, the company had been drawn into a classic U- or V-shaped enemy ambush. Jay Standish, operating in his capacity as the artillery forward observer to 2/9, noted that

VICTORY BETRAYED — Ronald Winter

while the Marines of Company G were traversing through nearly impenetrable jungle, the NVA *"were able to infiltrate along a nearby road, that was made of hard-packed earth."* As noted earlier by Miles Davis, the NVA knowledge of the terrain proved advantageous to their tactic of setting up ambushes, initiating fire fights and then disappearing into the jungle. The point fire team soon found itself pinned down amid approximately 30 NVA troops scattered in low-lying bunkers, and well-camouflaged among rocks and trees. Silhouetted against the sky if it attempted to withdraw, the team waited until the rest of the 3rd Platoon was brought up. The 2nd Platoon was then moved to the left, and as it started to sweep through the enemy position, came under a hail of automatic weapons and rocket propelled grenade (RPG) fire. With the 2nd and 3rd Platoons stopped, Hitzelberger ordered the 1st Platoon to swing further to the left and through a small ravine, flanking the enemy. By this maneuver, the 3rd Platoon was able to break through and force the NVA to withdraw. The company then pushed through the ambush site to a communications line where it consolidated its position. A cursory check of the immediate area revealed two enemy bodies and several blood trails. Five Marines were killed and 18 wounded. Among those who gave their lives during the battle was fire team leader Lance Corporal Thomas R Noonan, Jr., of Brooklyn, New York. During the fight, four of the wounded were exposed to enemy fire, and repeated attempts to recover them failed. However, Lance Corporal Noonan moved from his relatively secure position and maneuvered down the slope until he reached a spot near the injured Marines and took cover behind some rocks where he was heard shouting to encourage them. Ultimately, Noonan dashed from safety and commenced dragging the most seriously wounded man away from the fire-swept area. The citation for his actions states that, *"Although wounded and knocked to the ground by an enemy round, Lance*

Corporal Noonan recovered rapidly and resumed dragging the man toward the marginal security of a rock. He was, however, mortally wounded before he could reach his destination. His heroic actions inspired his fellow Marines to such aggressiveness that they initiated a spirited assault which forced the enemy soldiers to withdraw." Noonan was posthumously awarded the Medal of Honor for his daring efforts to rescue a seriously wounded fellow Marine.

NOONAN, THOMAS P., JR.

Rank and organization: Lance Corporal, U.S. Marine Corps, Company G, 2d Battalion, 9th Marines, 3d Marine Division. Place and Date: Near Vandergrift Combat Base, A Shau Valley, Republic of Vietnam, 5 February 1969. Entered service at: Brooklyn, N.Y. Born: 18 November 1943, Brooklyn, N.Y.

Citation:

For conspicuous gallantry and intrepidity at the risk of his life above and beyond the call of duty while serving as a fire team leader with Company G, in operations against the enemy in Quang Tri Province. Company G was directed to move from a position which they had been holding southeast of the Vandergrift Combat Base to an alternate location. As the Marines commenced a slow and difficult descent down the side of the hill made extremely slippery by the heavy rains, the leading element came under a heavy fire from a North Vietnamese Army unit occupying well-concealed positions in the rocky terrain. Four men were wounded, and repeated attempts to recover them failed because of the intense hostile fire. L/Cpl. Noonan moved from his position of relative security and, maneuvering down the treacherous slope to a location near the injured

men, took cover behind some rocks. Shouting words of encouragement to the wounded men to restore their confidence, he dashed across the hazardous terrain and commenced dragging the most seriously wounded man away from the fire-swept area. Although wounded and knocked to the ground by an enemy round, L/Cpl. Noonan recovered rapidly and resumed dragging the man toward the marginal security of a rock. He was, however, mortally wounded before he could reach his destination. His heroic actions inspired his fellow marines to such aggressiveness that they initiated a spirited assault which forced the enemy soldiers to withdraw. L/Cpl. Noonan's indomitable courage, inspiring initiative, and selfless devotion to duty upheld the highest traditions of the Marine Corps and the U.S. Naval Service. He gallantly gave his life for his country.[58]

With 30 minutes to reorganize for fear of a second attack, there was only time enough to destroy excess equipment and rig stretchers. At 1730, after putting out a strong rear guard and plotting artillery concentrations along the proposed route, the company moved down the ridge. The pace was slow and rest breaks frequent, as half the company was either assisting the walking wounded or carrying stretchers. Capt. Hitzelberger stated, *"The only way forward was down a sheer cliff with ropes. It took four hours just to get off the summit."*[59] Descending from the summit was like walking on a trail made of *"a rubber sheet covered with (vegetable) oil,"* Jay Standish recalled. *"Guys were moaning in pain and the NVA were taunting them in the dark all night."* Meanwhile, Cpl. Weber said, his squad *"remained in the rear of the column ... acting as a rear guard. When I finally moved down the hill with the squad, all I could see were the bodies of the dead and wounded."* Members of Weber's squad, *"carried one of the dead down the hill. (Two Marines) constructed a makeshift stretcher out of some tree limbs and vines. The dead Marine's face was not visible as someone had buttoned his shirt over the top of his head. I learned later it was the body of Private First Class Kenneth Jackson of Beckley, West Virginia. In addition to Noonan, the other Marines killed in action were Private First Class Robert McCluskey from Lowell, Massachusetts, and Lance Corporal Gary Haley from Marquette, Missouri. Fifth among the dead was one of our beloved Navy Corpsman, Bruce Bernstein, from Los Angeles, California."*

At 0200 the following morning, Capt. Hitzelberger decided to stop and settle in for the night even though the company was split because of a treacherous slope. The Marines established defensive positions as best they could in the dark, and spent the rest of the night on edge, waiting for attacks that never came. Early the next day, the company consolidated and began its trek toward a predetermined rendezvous with a relief platoon from Company E. The terrain, as before, proved to be a constant and major obstacle. *"The stretcher cases were moving up and down slopes in excess of 70 degrees,"* reported Capt. Hitzelberger. *"We had to use six, eight and, at times, 10 men to carry a stretcher, and it would take us over 30 minutes to move one stretcher case over one bad area."*[60] Infantryman Tom "Quick Draw" McGraw still remembers that descent decades later. *"Those were some of the worst days of my life,"* McGraw recalls. There was nothing easy or even merely difficult about the descent. The hill that took so much energy to ascend was even worse going back down with the dead and wounded. Marines who had been at a point of exhaustion a day earlier were moving as if automated, dealing at all times with slick mud, sharp rocks, cliffs, the cold, the rain, and ever-present threat of an NVA counterattack. At 1400, the company paused, and then began the most difficult part of its descent. During the next several hours, Marines roped the stretchers and wounded down the face of a rocky cliff without incident. At the bottom the company linked up with the relief platoon which had brought out medical supplies and the first rations the Marines had had in three days. For the next 36 hours, the company wound its way down Hill 1175 toward the river. Despite the incredible difficulties encountered, *"We never gave up and brought all Marines off that mountain,"* McGraw said. *"I'm so proud to have been a part of that company of Marines."* McGraw said he thinks of that fight and the descent off Hill 1175 every February. *"Strange, even after all these years the memories still come back every year,"* he noted.

When Company G finally made it to the Da Krong on 7 February, Marine aircrews made a heroic effort to extract the most seriously wounded. In dense fog, and after having been fired on from the high ground during their approach, two medical evacuation helicopters from HMM-161 flew up the Da Krong, using the river as their guide. Piloting the lead helicopter in the two-aircraft section was Capt. Gary Freese, who had picked up gunship support from two US Army UH-1 Hueys on the way into the valley. *"It was the only time in my tour that the Army flew as escorts,"* Freese remembered, but he was nonetheless happy to have help suppressing the NVA fire. Freese had flown the A Shau many times before, but on this mission he made the approach under extremely hazardous conditions, flying just above the Da Krong River with a 500-foot ceiling. *"We had worked out a flight escape plan for flying in the fog, but we maintained VFR (Visual Flight Reference) for the whole mission,"* Freese said. Landing zones in the area were locked in by cloud cover. To avoid the clouds Company G Marines had carried the dead and wounded to a lower elevation which required Freese to land in the river. Freese selected a large flat boulder that was near a waterfall, but also had just enough room to give his rear wheels a stable platform. Freese remembers being

71

VICTORY BETRAYED — Ronald Winter

literally adjacent to the waterfall, which provided sufficient room for the second helicopter to settle in.

In the cabin of the aircraft Crew Chief Cpl. Ed Irwin dropped the ramp, made his way outside and motioned for the Marines on shore to begin loading. A steady stream of stretcher bearers brought the most seriously wounded out to the aircraft that was perched precariously on the boulder adjacent to the waterfall. As he had done myriad times before in the nine months he had been crewing in-country, Irwin counted the stretchers, halting the procession when the aircraft reached maximum capacity. But this time, things were different. Irwin was tasked with managing the procession of wounded into an aircraft that was perched on a boulder in the bottom of what essentially was a very narrow V, with the jungle coming right down to the river and tree limbs dangerously close to the rotor blades. The noise of the rotors, plus the screaming jet engines right over his head, not to mention the roar of the waterfall, made verbal communication all but impossible. In virtually every other medevac mission he had flown, stretcher bearers entered the aircraft on the rear ramp, set the stretchers down, and then exited a cabin door on the starboard side further forward, just behind the cockpit. But what no one told Irwin, and what could have turned a successful mission into a tragedy, was that most of the stretcher bearers also were casualties who were setting the stretchers down, and then taking a seat themselves. The Super D model of the CH-46 carried a maximum of 25 passengers[61] under normal circumstances, but that number fluctuated greatly depending on altitude, temperature and humidity. Regardless, when Irwin believed he had reached capacity and hit the remote button on his crew-chief's *"long cord"* that closed the ramp as he entered the cabin, he was horrified to see the interior jam-packed with wounded Marines, including stretcher cases and ambulatory. In the cockpit Freese already was putting power to the engines and attempting to lift, while grossly overloaded. Nearly five decades later, Irwin, still the consummate professional, put the blame for the situation squarely on his own shoulders. But simply put, Irwin was the victim of non-existent communication in a hot zone, with dozens of lives on the line. Irwin didn't have the room to roam outside his aircraft to ensure that proper procedures were being observed, and the crew members inside the cabin didn't know that Irwin didn't know the cabin was full to overflowing. Yet for all that could have happened, what did happen is that Freese coaxed the aircraft off the boulder, out of the river and away from the battle. It could have been that regardless of what the flight manuals said, the engineers back at Boeing Vertol who designed the CH-46 put a little extra power in the engines and a little more lift into the blades, for just such situations that arise in the *"fog of war."* Or, it could have been Freese's superb flying skills that got the CH-46 airborne. Whatever the reason, the 46 lifted off the boulder, gained altitude, and began making its way back to higher level medical facilities. And what Irwin couldn't hear, but what Jay Standish, clearly remembers, is that when Irwin's aircraft began ascending, with the second aircraft right behind, 100 Marine infantrymen were only yards away in the jungle cheering their hearts out. They had fought a brutal battle and brought their dead and wounded back from the battlefield in the most difficult of situations. They cheered from relief, they cheered because they knew the dead from their unit would be returned home for proper burials, and the wounded would now receive the medical care they needed.

But even as the cheers died out in the dense jungle, the mission wasn't over for the crews of the CH-46 helicopters that pulled off such a dramatic rescue. Cpl. Jeff Harnly, a Minnesota native

VICTORY BETRAYED — Ronald Winter

trained as a helicopter avionics technician, who also flew regularly as a machine gunner, remembers looking intently out the window at the starboard gunner's station, trying to spot telltale muzzle flashes or smoke rings from the NVA. What he saw instead, hiding in the jungle only a matter of yards from where Company G Marines were preparing to finish the journey to FSB Dallas, *was a wild boar. It must have weighed 400 pounds.* Harnly was no stranger to the wildlife that inhabited Vietnam's jungles. Only two months earlier he had been flying gunner on a similar mission, a medevac further north where the Demilitarized Zone met the Laotian border. The mission was initially reported as a nighttime emergency extraction of a wounded Marine recon, but as the aircraft settled into a low hover just above a shell crater where the recon team had set up a defensive perimeter, the crew discovered that the Marine was wounded not by the enemy but by a 300-pound Bengal Tiger that had mauled him. The other members of the patrol had pulled the Marine from the tiger's jaws and killed the beast. The tiger's carcass soon joined the wounded Marine and the rest of the patrol for the ride back to Quang Tri. In the jungle further south during Operation Dewey Canyon, relatives of that tiger were never far from the Marines, whether on patrol or in the base camps. *"We could hear them roaring in the jungle, and down in the valleys,"* Standish recalled. During the 7 February medevac the wild boar was dangerously close to the Marines but caused no problems for their return to FSB Dallas.

On the Dewey Canyon extraction, Harnly was not the only observer of Vietnamese fauna. Cpl. Dan Haire, crew chief of the chase aircraft, also had a wildlife moment literally in the same area as Harnly. Haire's aircraft carried all of Company G's dead, always a somber occurrence for Marine air crews. But they still were in a hot zone, and Haire, like Harnly in the lead aircraft, turned his attention to the terrain below and the possibility of seeing an NVA position. Looking out at the jungle as his aircraft lifted off, he saw not a wild boar, but *"a huge ape-like creature,"* in the treetops beneath him. Exactly what Haire glimpsed is not known. He could have seen a relative of the so-called "Rock Apes" that Marines had encountered in the region since they first entered northern I Corps in force. Or, Haire may have been one of the first outsiders to see what in 2011 was declared to be a new species of primate dubbed the Northern Buffed-Cheeked Gibbon that lives in the area where Dewey Canyon was conducted.[62] Regardless, both aircraft cleared the river landing zone carrying all the dead and wounded from Company G's battle on Co Ka Leuye, Hill 1175. They made it back, first to Vandegrift and ultimately Provisional MAG 39 in Quang Tri, with only one bullet hole in one rotor blade, despite the enemy fire. *"It was a grueling flight,"* Freese recalled. But even with all the difficulties they encountered and those that could have been, Freese believes he arrived at that place, at that moment, *"at the right time in terms of flying experience."* Freese was later awarded the Distinguished Flying Cross for the heroism shown in that flight.

On 8 February, Company G returned to FSB Dallas. The ordeal, as Lieutenant Colonel George C. Fox later noted, *"was a tremendous performance in leadership and fire discipline ... I went out and talked to those young Marines as they came in, every last one of them. They were smiling and laughing. Their clothes were torn, and in some cases completely off of them, but they were ready for a fight."* [63]

The weather continued to be a problem for several more days in mid-February and sporadically throughout the operation. The two ARVN battalions on FSB Lightning experienced their own weather difficulties right from the start. As the weather closed in on 1 February the battalions' direct support artillery battery and remaining supplies were in the process of being inserted. By the time all helicopter operations halted, only one of the six 105mm howitzers and 400 rounds of ammunition had been delivered. The battalions themselves carried only the basic allowance supplied to each infantryman.

With conventional resupply out of the question, it was decided to attempt a helicopter-parachute drop by directing two CH-46s over the target with the assistance of the Vandegrift Air Support Radar Team (ASRT). The ASRT employed a radar-course-directing central computer which consisted of precision radar and associated computer equipment designed to accurately position aircraft without visual reference to the earth's surface.[64] Both drops landed within 100 meters of the ARVN position, even though the team's radar equipment was operating beyond its normal range.[65]

The helicopter supply drops were one of the methods that the air commanders developed to offset the impasse established by the monsoons. From 5 to 8 February, Marine fixed-wing KC-130s made additional ASRT-controlled drops adjacent to Marine positions. Although the "Hercules" could drop greater quantities of supplies, the drops proved to be less accurate, and the percentage of loads recovered fell from 80 to 66.[66]

1st Lt. Fred Penning a section leader with HMM-161 took part in the supply drops during that period and remembers finishing the early morning briefings during Operation Dewey Canyon's worst weather. *"You walked out the door and you could almost touch the clouds,"* he said. *"The helicopter pilots thus used radio frequencies from Dong Ha and Quang Tri to get in the vicinity of the drop area."* Using the TACAN (Tactical Air Navigation) systems they could get the proper headings and distances. *"We were trained to fly instruments, but not like modern commercial pilots,"* he said. The resupply flights would lift off in sections of four helicopters, with five-minute intervals between sections to provide sufficient separation. Despite the application of Distance Measuring Equipment, and radio contact with the troops on the ground, the supply drops were still *"very inexact,"* Penning said. *"We'd climb through the junk, get on top, and drop the chutes or kick the stuff out,"* he recalled. The drops had to be close to the Marines, but not too close to avoid inadvertently hitting troops on the ground. Yet they couldn't be too far away, or the supplies could be captured by the NVA before the Marines could find them. Overall, the system worked but not without its share of gallows humor. *"More than, once I'd get a radio message telling me 'You broke my crackers again,'"* Penning said.

These initial experiences led to a refinement of the Vandegrift facilities and the installation of a second ASRT team at Cunningham on 26 February. Working together, they provided extended radar coverage, increasing the accuracy of subsequent resupply drops, and the regiment's counter-battery capability during night missions and inclement weather.[67]

Another innovation also paid high dividends in the handling of casualties in the field when bad weather precluded helicopter medical evacuations. In November 1968, the regimental and three battalion surgeons had developed and fabricated a helicopter-transportable aid station, capable of providing maximum lifesaving care as field conditions would allow. One such aid station accompanied the 9th Marines to Cunningham and was placed into full operation soon after the fire support base opened. During the first week of February, when the weather would not permit helicopter evacuation of casualties, the Cunningham station proved invaluable in the number of lives saved.[68]

For many of the units, the resupply situation was becoming dire. Wilkes remembers talking with one infantryman, *"who had no rounds for his M-16. He had a big pile of rocks by his position, and told me facetiously, 'I've got about 20 rounds here.'"*

VICTORY BETRAYED — Ronald Winter

"If we hadn't been resupplied," Col. Wilkes remembered, *"in many positions, we were defenseless."*

Ultimately the socked-in monsoon weather lasted nine days, interrupting the regiment's forward progress, and giving enemy units the opportunity to reposition, prepare their own defenses, and offensive maneuvers as well. The enemy had figured out the extent of the Marine offensive, and where it was headed. The NVA used the lull to plan attacks against the Marine firebases. If the NVA could eliminate the firebases, they could seriously hamper the Marines' ability to move forward with covering artillery fire when necessary. By 10 February, the weather cleared sufficiently for helicopters to move units of the 1st Battalion, 9th Marines from Vandegrift and Shiloh to FSB Erskine, and Battery F from Razor to Erskine. With all battalions in place, the stage was now set for the southward drive across the Da Krong.[69]

AUTHOR'S OBSERVATIONS

Who Ruled What?

A line in the Billy Joel song Goodnight Saigon, says *"We held the day in the palm of our hands. They ruled the night ... "*

Bull! That may have been true in the initial stages of the Vietnam War when newly arrived American troops were fighting local Viet Cong guerilla units, comprised mainly of local communists, or their conscripts, who lived their entire lives in the areas where they were fighting.

But American forces steadily decimated those units and the North Vietnamese communists soon ran out of local replacements. Meaning the Viet Cong had to import reinforcements from areas further away–they had no more idea of the lay of the land than the allied forces they were facing. In essence, they were as blind in the dark as US forces, except that many of our troops developed excellent night vision and had the upper hand there too. In time, especially after the Tet Offensive of February 1968, the Viet Cong essentially did not exist as a viable fighting force. With so many NVA troops being killed each year, the only viable replacements were North Vietnamese conscripts and Chinese mercenaries. By 1968, the free-world forces ruled the day and the night while engaged with the communists, and North Vietnamese regular units could just as easily walk into a night ambush set up by US troops, as the Americans would have four years earlier when fighting local Viet Cong.

AUTHOR'S OBSERVATIONS

Joe and the Tiger

Ask anyone who served in the northern I Corps area of Vietnam, especially those who patrolled the mountainous terrain near the Laotian border and the Demilitarized Zone, and they'll tell you *"Yeah, I heard about those tigers. They'd sneak right up on the grunts and kill them on the spot."*

Which actually was true. In late 1968 the situation erupted, and in the midst of the fighting, a team of hunters—no kidding, hunters—was dispatched into that remote area to find and kill at least one of the offending beasts.

I flew gunner on a flight that took the hunters to the area. It was one of the strangest missions I ever flew—considering that the rifles carried by the passengers were hunting rifles, not standard military battle rifles. Taking a hunting team out into a war zone just looked strange and unsettling—as if everything was just out of place.

Nearly 50 years later the subject came up repeatedly at reunions of the air crews who served in that area. The discussions prompted Joseph Carcasio—a New Jersey native who flew with HMM-161 and was a gunner on one tiger flight—to document the story of the crew that rescued a Marine recon, who had been attacked one night while on patrol. But nearly as soon as he began his research, Joe ran into issues, starting with two sets of memories that conflicted on what happened. It took a little time and sorting out but Joe finally got to the truth. There were two sets of stories because there had been two different attacks, close in time and place, but separate.

81

In one, where Joe was a gunner, the recon was attacked as he settled into a night defensive position. His teammates killed the tiger and called for a medevac. The team was in a shell hole on a ridge that sloped into jungle on one side and had a cliff on the other side—the side where Joe was the gunner. Pilot Gene Massey kept the aircraft in a hover a couple of feet off the ground in dense fog, and gunner Jeff Harnly, who was on the only side where an attack could be launched, manned his machine gun. Meanwhile co-pilot Terry Powell, crew-chief Chuck Palmer and Joe, went out the rear and helped the recon team get their teammate inside the aircraft, and then joined forces to lift a dead 300-lb tiger in as well. That is the definition of a really scary and highly unusual mission. In the other, a tiger stalked a Marine infantryman who was on patrol, in the rear guard position. In that instance, the tiger attacked and killed the Marine, and the hunting team went out to settle the score. Joe wrote up a paper on the tale of the tigers, and even designed a limited-edition Challenge Coin especially for the crews who had flown those missions.

IN PURSUIT OF THE NVA

"Battalion commanders went right along with [their troops],
no jeeps obviously, or any of that nonsense."

The 3rd Battalion, 9th Marines crossed the Song Da Krong early on the morning of 11 February, initiating Phase III of Operation Dewey Canyon. The 1st and 2nd Battalions followed the next day. Each battalion was given a zone of action approximately five kilometers wide and an objective about eight kilometers south southwest of the point of departure. To the east, the 3rd Battalion was to attack along ridgelines 2,000 meters apart, with one company securing Hill 1228 (Tiger Mountain), and two companies taking Hill 1224 (Tam Boi).

The 1st Battalion was to advance over two parallel ridgelines further west, converging on a single objective astride the Laotian border. On the regiment's western flank, the 2nd Battalion was to attack through a broad valley with secondary assaults on the ridges to the east. The battalion's final objective also lay on the South Vietnamese-Laotian border. Tactically, Colonel Barrow divided each battalion: two companies attacking along parallel ridgelines with two companies in trace. The lead company was to attack and if heavily engaged, the company in trace, or its platoons, was to act as the maneuver element, assisting the attacking company and securing a landing zone for resupply and medical evacuation, if necessary. When the situation permitted, the company in trace would assume the lead and the company in the attack would fall back. The scheme of movement, according to Barrow, *"was masterfully done. Battalion commanders went right along with [their troops], no jeeps obviously, or any of that nonsense."* As each battalion moved across Phase Line Red, it made strong contact. Three companies of Lieutenant Colonel George W. Smith's 1st Battalion (The Walking Dead) immediately encountered a sizeable enemy force which had apparently been positioned to mount a ground attack against FSB Erskine. Assisted by the well-aimed fire of five artillery batteries, the Marines forced the enemy to withdraw, leaving behind 25 killed in addition to numerous weapons, packs, and explosives.[70]

Meanwhile, further east, Company M threw back a mortar-supported ground attack by an estimated NVA platoon, killing 18 while losing two Marines. After fighting a day-long series of minor skirmishes on 13 February, Company C collided with a mortar-and-machine-gun-reinforced enemy platoon deployed on a hilltop in a line defense. The ensuing Marine assault forced the enemy from the hill, killing 12 NVA. That night, the Marines employed mortars and artillery to break an enemy effort to retake the hill, claiming an additional 12 NVA during the battle. Company C losses for the day were two killed and 21 wounded. The opposition the Marines found themselves up against was determined and formidable. Enemy forces, unlike those encountered during Phase II, were well-disciplined and remained in their bunkers or fighting holes until overrun or destroyed. At night they would probe or attack Marine company positions using squads or platoons. These suicide techniques seemed to be designed for only one purpose: to prevent or delay the Marines' advance on Route 922 (the Ho Chi Minh Trail), along with the important supply area and artillery positions which encircled it. The enemy's tough resistance achieved little success. Employing a heavy volume of accurate artillery fire and air strikes, the three battalions advanced steadily southward. Attesting to the performance of Marine firepower, two 122mm field guns were destroyed on 15 February—one by air, the other by artillery.[71]

VICTORY BETRAYED — Ronald Winter

Marine scout-sniper teams also contributed to the success of the attack by shooting their NVA counterparts out of trees on several occasions. Accompanying some of the advancing Marines were scout dog teams that were invaluable in alerting the troops to hidden enemy. Despite the Marine successes it also was apparent that the NVA soldiers were withdrawing into Laos. From the outset of the American involvement in Vietnam, the North Vietnamese leadership in Hanoi considered all of what had been French Indochina, including Vietnam, Laos and Cambodia, to be the battlefield. In Washington, D.C., thousands of miles away, for political reasons, the decision had been made to confine American ground forces to South Vietnam. Incursions into neighboring Laos or Cambodia (except for Special Operations) were forbidden.[72]

That was a situation made to order for the NVA. If pressed and hammered too hard, the NVA simply could step across the border into Laos and enjoy an undisturbed breathing spell. The 9th Marines could only sit, handcuffed on the Vietnamese side of the border.[73]

AUTHOR'S OBSERVATIONS

Red Rover, Red Rover, Send a SOG Team Over

There were many issues faced by the Americans who fought in the Vietnam War, most of which have been relegated to the concept of "handcuffing" the troops and making it virtually impossible to accomplish the mission of forcing the communists to surrender.

Chief amongst these issues was the existence and use of various forms of Special Operations units, whose primary and unenviable job was to cross the Laotian border and get as close as possible to North Vietnamese forces to see what they were doing. This type of extremely hazardous reconnaissance gathering provided the best information on troop movements, weaponry and related matters. These duties were carried out by Marine Recons, Navy SEALS, Army Long Range Reconnaissance teams, Army Rangers, and Special Operations Group teams, among others.

During Operation Dewey Canyon as the 9th Marines pushed closer and closer to the Laotian border, SOG teams were also operating in the area, leading to considerable interaction between the two forces. Marine helicopter crews often were dispatched across the border to reinforce or extract SOG teams that were engaged with communist forces. This brings up the issue of the Rules of Engagement. Helicopter crews who were prevented from crossing the Laotian border for routine resupply or medevac missions, were permitted to insert or extract SOG teams.

If that seems nonsensical, and begs the question of just who was interpreting the ROEs back in the States, imagine what the troops must have been thinking out in the jungle.

PHOTOS & MAPS

NOTE:

To better present the details of these photos and maps, we placed the landscape oriented images so that the picture is shown at it's largest possible size. The reader needs only to turn the book sideways to see them easily.

Many of these photos were taken during the actual events of Operation Dewey Canyon, and were reproduced from original hard copy photos 45 years after the end of the Vietnam War in 1975.

Figure 1. Dewey Canyon Area of Operations
(Public Domain)

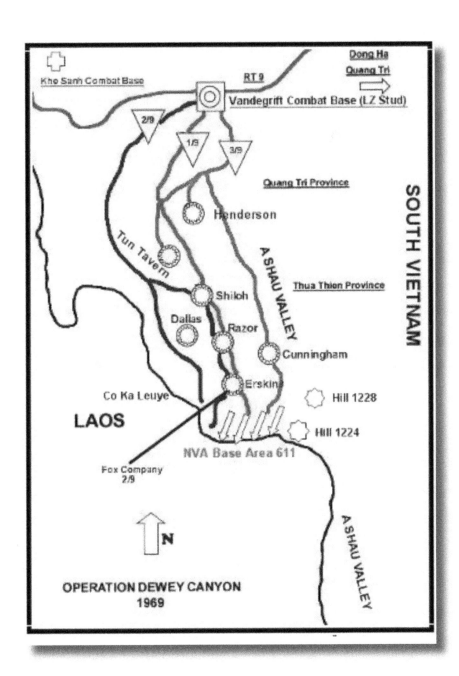

Kho Sanh Combat Base

RT 9

Dong Ha
Quang Tri

Vandegrift Combat Base (LZ Stud)

2/9

1/9

3/9

Quang Tri Province

Henderson

Tun Tavern

A SHAU VALLEY

Thua Thien Province

Shiloh

Dallas

Razor

Cunningham

Erskine

Co Ka Leuye

Hill 1228

LAOS

Hill 1224

NVA Base Area 611

Fox Company
2/9

SOUTH VIETNAM

A SHAU VALLEY

N

OPERATION DEWEY CANYON
1969

Figure 2. A section of Rt.922, the Ho Chi Minh Trail in Laos during Operation Dewey Canyon. Capt. Jay Standish photo.

Figure 3. Leatherneck Square outlines 1967.
(Public Domain)

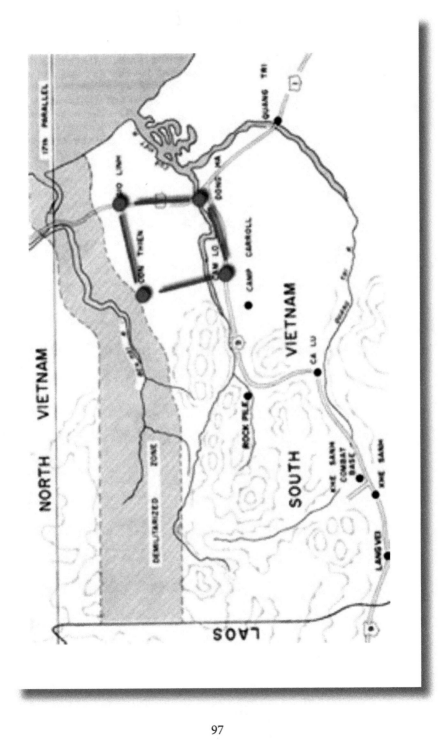

Figure 4. Gen. Raymond G. "Razor" Davis 1971-72
Asst. Commandant.
USMC photo.

Figure 5. A portion of Provisional Marine Air Group 39 Quang Tri.

101

Figure 6. CH-46 Ds at lifting off from Vandegrift Combat Base.

Figure 7. Recons entering the bush.

Figure 8. Dispirited communist soldiers take a break on the Ho Chi Minh Trail before resuming their march to the south where hardships, a hostile populous, and a good possibility of being wounded or killed await them.

Figure 9. A CH-53 helicopter delivers water to the field in Vietnam. Popasmoke photo.

Figure 10. A .50 caliber anti-aircraft gun captured during Operation Dewey Canyon. Capt. Jay Standish photo.

Figure 11. Marines examine NVA communication wire.
Capt. Jay Standish photo.

Figure 12. Co Ka Leuye Hill 1175 from the approach. Capt. Jay Standish photo.

Figure 13. Marines fighting their way to Co Ka Leuye. Operation Dewey Canyon. Capt. Jay Standish photo.

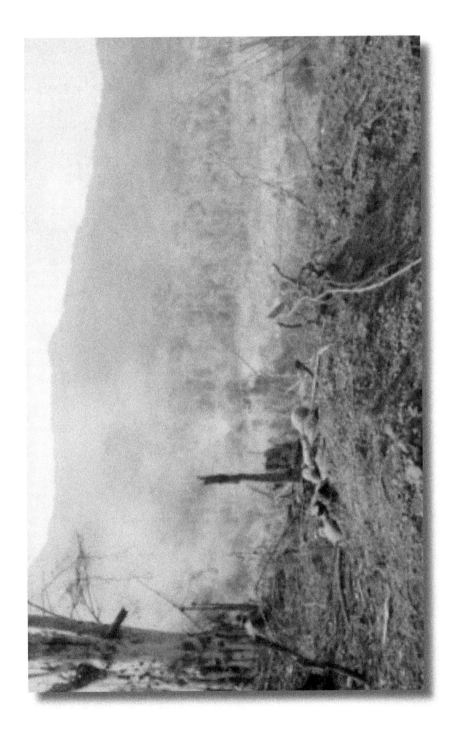

Figure 14. A CH-46 Super D helicopter flies over the Da Krong River under a very low ceiling on Operation Dewey Canyon. Bob Odom photo.

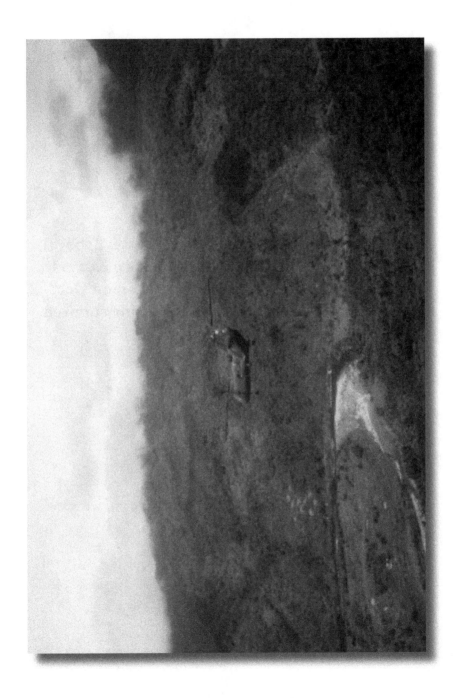

Figure 15. HMM-161 pilots Gene Massey (above) and Terry Powell examine the remains of a 300 lb. Bengal Tiger that mauled a Marine recon on Dec. 22, 1968 in Quang Tri Province. The Marine survived. Jeff Harnly photo.

Figure 16. Tiger Mountain Hill 1228 near the Ho Chi Minh trail. Bob Odom photo.

Figure 17. Marines guard a Russian-made 122mm artillery piece captured during Operation Dewey Canyon. Capt. Jay Standish photo.

125

Figure 18. Col. Harvey C. Barnum
USMC photo.

Figure 19. Cpl. James Johnson on Operation Dewey Canyon. Capt. Jay Standish photo.

Figure 20. Lt. Bob Odom a CH-46 pilot with HMM-161, takes a break on a Russian 122mm artillery piece captured in Operation Dewey Canyon. Bob Odom photo.

Figure 21. This dense jungle foliage was a constant obstacle on Operation Dewey Canyon. A Marine peering through the bush can barely be seen.
Capt. Jay Standish photo.

Figure 22. CH-54 Skycrane lifting two UH-1 Huey helicopters. (Public Domain)

Figure 23. Dragonfly—Nature's inspiring shape for the CH-54 Skycrane. Andre Karwath photo.

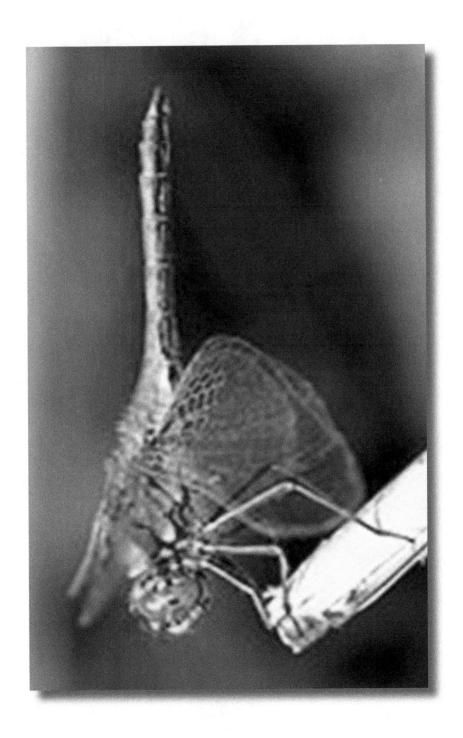

Figure 24. Rt. 922 in Laos near Base Area 611. Capt. Jay Standish photo.

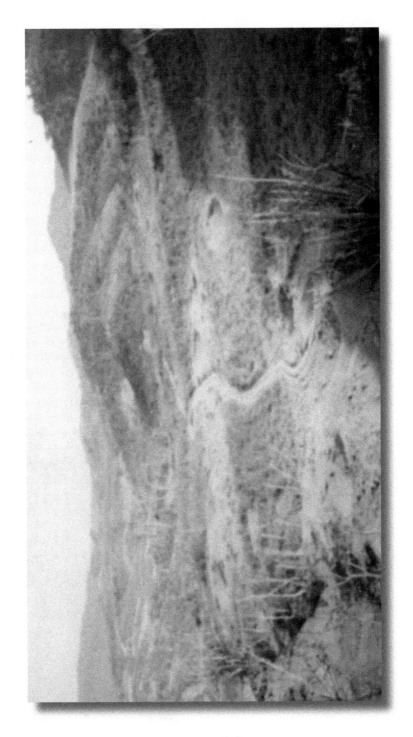

Figure 25. Russian Truck destroyed in Laos ambush.
Capt. Jay Standish photo.

Figure 26. Marines of the 2nd Battalion, 9th Marines inspect a weapons cache left behind by retreating North Vietnamese communists. Capt. Jay Standish photo.

Figure 27. Russian-made 122mm artillery piece captured in Laos during Operation Dewey Canyon. Capt. Jay Standish photo.

145

Figure 28. An abandoned NVA bunker along Rt. 922, the Ho Chi Minh Trail in Laos, February 1969. Capt. Jay Standish photo.

Figure 29. A Marine scout from the 2nd Battalion, 9th Marines with a South Vietnamese Kit Carson scout on the Ho Chi Minh Trail in Operation Dewey Canyon. Capt. Jay Standish photo.

Figure 30. Company E Marines, 2nd Battalion, 9th Marines take five on the Ho Chi Minh trail, Laos, Feb. 1969. Capt. Jay Standish photo.

Figure 31. Jay Standish on Ho Chi Minh Trail in Laos shortly after promotion to 1st Lieutenant. Capt. Jay Standish photo.

153

Figure 32. Maj. James S. Loop Quang Tri RVN 1968.

Figure 33. Col. (ret.) Warren Wiedhahn with a shell casing from a Russian 122mm cannon captured in Operation Dewey Canyon.

Figure 34. William H. Sullivan, center, former Ambassador to Laos, with Henry Kissinger, left, Secretary of State in the Nixon Administration. Washington Post photo.

Figure 35. Lieutenant General Dong Sy Nguyen, commander of the Ho Chi Minh Trail for 8 years until the war ended in 1975. Notably, Col. Bui Tin, who served on the General Staff of North Vietnam's army, received the unconditional surrender of South Vietnam on 30 April 1975, and later became editor of the People's Daily, remarked, "If Johnson had granted General William Westmoreland's requests to enter Laos and block the Ho Chi Minh trail, Hanoi could not have won the war."

INSPECTION ARMS

"I was a hunter and a killer.
That's exactly what a Marine rifleman does in combat.
I was there to find the enemy, close with the enemy, and kill the enemy."

During periods of extended combat there can be certain relaxations of rules and regulations regarding the status of uniforms, usually because the weather, terrain and enemy contacts make it virtually impossible to maintain an inspection-ready appearance. Such was the case with Capt. Harvey Barnum's E Battery of the 12th Marines. Barnum, a recipient of the Medal of Honor for heroism in combat in his first Vietnam tour in 1965, recalled decades later that he had been deeply involved with the layout of Fire Support Base Cunningham. His command, E Battery, was situated in the most remote section of the base—the furthest from headquarters. With so many fire missions—virtually non-stop it seemed—and the scarcity of basic necessities such as water for shaving, Barnum allowed E Battery gunners to engage in a mustache growing contest. Barnum, it should be noted, joined in. But on February 15 Capt. Barnum took a tour of his battery with the company gunnery sergeant, checking with each Marine as to the condition of his position, his weapons, other gear, and speaking with them to ascertain whether there were any personal or morale problems. Barnum recalls being *"professionally pissed"* to find many men without proper equipment, or side arms that needed cleaning, and other lapses. The artillery pieces were well maintained and in excellent firing order, but a few steps away things were in less than desirable shape. By the next morning he had gone through the entire battery, replacing missing or damaged equipment. *"The men were bitching,"* Barnum recalled, but in two days the requirement for personnel readiness would be all too clear.[74]

VICTORY BETRAYED — Ronald Winter

Sharp clashes across the entire front marked the action on 16 and 17 February. On the left flank, Company K, 3rd Battalion, moving toward an intermediate objective, was attacked from the front and rear by an unknown number of North Vietnamese troops. Using all available supporting arms to silence enemy mortar and rocket-propelled grenade fire (RPG), the company killed 17 communists and seized a number of weapons in taking the position, while sustaining few casualties. In observance of Tet—the Lunar New Year celebrated across much of Asia—the North Vietnamese and Viet Cong unilaterally declared a weeklong truce. The allied countrywide 24-hour truce went into effect at 1800 on 16 February. But as Major Joseph B. Knotts, the regimental operations officer, commented, *"Out on Dewey Canyon you wouldn't know there was any."* In the early morning hours on 17 February the enemy began hitting the base with a pre-planned mortar barrage. The NVA had kept the base under surveillance for nearly a week from the dense jungle nearby, and their incoming fire hit with pinpoint accuracy.[75] Lt. John Cochenour, Executive Officer of E battery, 2nd Battalion, 12th Marines recalled that the battery had ceased fire at midnight. *"I caught a short hour or so of sleep. Generators were running to provide power farther up the ridge at the HQ units, so there was a background buzz, but otherwise it was dark and fairly quiet."* That quiet didn't last for long, and Cochenour remembered that as the mortars began dropping, *"I dropped to the ground and begin to crawl back towards the Number 2 gun pit, when a round hit the powder box on gun 1, and a fire flared up followed by an explosion caused by another mortar, an RPG, or a satchel charge. The explosion knocked me aside and showered me with dirt and debris, and generally rang my bell. I would hear much of the next hour's fighting as through a bucket. In the light of the fire in the gun pit I could see running men silhouetted, and small arms fire began to erupt from the perimeter infantry and my own gun pits."* As captured documents were later to show, the NVA set up a short distance away in the nearly impenetrable jungle and mapped out access and egress routes, minefield locations and patrol patterns. The monsoon rain that had forced the Marines to curtail offensive operations also provided cover for the NVA. As the mortar barrage continued, a 200-man NVA force consisting of 100 sappers, backed by 100 infantrymen made their way stealthily through the night hidden by a dense fog. Dressed in shorts, skullcaps, and weighted down with explosives, the NVA infiltrated through the base garbage dump and using well-worn paths back to each unit's position, broke through the defensive wire and dashed toward the center of the fire support base, tossing concussion grenades and satchel charges into every open hole. Although initially caught by surprise, the Marines of Company L, securing the fire support base, quickly organized a drive to clear the base in the face of heavy enemy mortar and recoilless rifle fire. Lieutenant Colonel Joseph R. Scoppa's 2nd Battalion, 12th Marines bore the brunt of the attack. Within the first minutes the Fire Direction Center was put out of action, as was one howitzer from E Battery.[76]

The loss of the FDC was no small matter. Without it there were major gaps in the process of ordering return fire. Without the pinpoint accuracy that the process provided, or if there was a mistake anywhere along the way, shells could go far off target, or fall into friendly troops' positions. But the batteries also were trained in self-defensive measures should the FDC be damaged or destroyed. And there was a tangible element of ingenuity on Operation Dewey Canyon, due primarily to the people of the 9th and 12th Marines. In the case of the sapper attack on FSB Cunningham, one example of that ingenuity in the opening moments came from then-Capt. Barnum, who quickly ascended a raised observation position he had constructed next to his command bunker, just for a situation that currently was at hand. Coordinating with the infantry, he ordered battery howitzers to lower their barrels and fire *"beehive"* rounds directly into the attacking forces. Firing beehive rounds containing thousands of sharp darts, or fleshettes, usually required a request that went up the chain of command to the battalion CO, and then back down again to the requesting battery. In this case, however, *"I counted to 10 and we let loose on the NVA,"* Barnum said.[77] As the ferocious fighting continued, the concept that *"every Marine is a rifleman first,"* came into play as a reaction force of clerks, cooks, radio operators and engineers began a systematic drive to eliminate the enemy forces within the perimeter. The cooks from I Battery accounted for 13 enemy killed when they manned a .50-caliber machine gun.[78] The Marines of E Battery fought back ferociously, as did every Marine on the base, and due to Barnum's inspection of E battery little more than a day earlier, his troops did not lack for operational rifles and side arms to assist in the damage being wrought by the battery's artillery.

Lt. Cochenour, back at the XO's bunker, found the Marine assigned as a battery recorder, *"on the wire talking to the guns. We had lost the link to guns number 1 and 2, as well as communications with the centralized fire direction center."* The recorder became a messenger and ran between E and D batteries until the central FDC came online again about 30 minutes later, when the battalion re-established centralized fire control. Throughout the night they expended 3,270 rounds including 147 beehive rounds fired directly into what Barnum described as *"human wave"* attacks. Also in support, the ARVN 105mm battery on FSB Lightning unleashed reinforcing fires totaling 340 rounds. When radioing to the ARVN battery for support, the Marines on FSB Cunningham literally became Forward Observers, calling in strikes on or near their own positions. In addition, *"Our battery gun line was drilled in self-defensive action, and each gun section fired illumination rounds and firecracker rounds against the west mountain face, while manning small arms throughout each gun pit,"* Cochenour said. With the sun up in the morning sky at the close of the action, the air was heavy with dust and the powders from propellants and explosives. Odors hung in the air from hot gun barrels, sweat, and blood. *"It seemed still and surreal to me,"* Cochenour said. *"We had lost gun number one, and the gun position was unrecognizable. A few bodies of sappers were dragged down to a collection point. Our battery had four wounded Marines, three from gun one."* [79] A sweep of the base and surrounding hillsides at first light revealed 37 NVA bodies, 13 of which were within the perimeter. As John Wilkes recalls, the attack was chaotic, brutal, and some NVA at one point came *"within 50 feet of Col. Barrow."* But they were stopped. As with most other engagements in Dewey Canyon the communist losses were likely much higher than reported. A ring of artillery fire lasted throughout the fighting blasting troop concentrations, escape routes and other targets of opportunity that unquestionably added to the enemy death toll. In addition, as Barnum and others recalled, *"there were body parts all over the place,"* from the exploding artillery, including beehive rounds that literally tore the attackers to pieces. Many individual weapons, grenades, and packs were also located, the latter containing invaluable intelligence in the form of orders, tactics, and maps used to prepare the assault, as well as quantities of marijuana and other drugs. The use of narcotics, Second Lieutenant Milton J. Teixeira explained, *"made them a lot harder to kill. Not one of the NVA we had inside the perimeter had less than three or four holes in him. Usually it took a grenade or something to stop him completely."* [80] Four Marines were killed and 46 were wounded during the fight. By 0800 the job of repairing the damage was well underway. There also was the issue of medical evacuations for the wounded and beginning the long journey home for the deceased.

However, the same dense fog that made the assault possible the previous night, now made it impossible for helicopters to locate the landing zone and begin the evacuations. Nonetheless, a solution was at hand. The Air Liaison Officer assigned to the 9th Marines for Operation Dewey Canyon, Major Fred Gatz, was on FSB Cunningham and immediately stepped up to find a way—unconventional though it may have seemed—to get the evacuation and resupply helicopters in. Gatz was a helicopter pilot with HML-367 when the opportunity presented itself to help improve the communications between ground and airborne forces. He volunteered in the early fall of 1968, was selected and assigned to the 9th Marines. Gatz saw Dewey Canyon as a major opportunity to help make battle support more effective and efficient, and he considered Col. Barrow to be, *"the finest Marine I have ever known. A real southern gentleman."* Despite the negative media at the time that was often condescending about the intellectual capabilities of the military in general, and military leadership in particular, Gatz was impressed to learn that Col. Barrow carried a copy of Thucydides' <u>The History of the Peloponnesian War</u> in his pack and studied it regularly. With the leadership and improvisational capabilities of Col. Barrow and Major Gen. Davis as models, Gatz set to figuring a way to solve the weather dilemma. The solution was literally all around him. As noted previously, when an artillery piece fires a projectile, it uses a varying number of bags of powder charges to launch the round. Each round for the 105mm howitzers came with 7 bags of powder for the charge, and the canisters were packed with the requisite number of powder bags for the mission at hand. Often, with closer targets, there were several bags left over that were to be disposed of under strict weather conditions and control. In this case, the unused bags had been accumulating and some were even used to mark the boundaries of the LZ. Gatz assembled a crew that began collecting the unused powder bags, as well as ammunition crates, pallets, C-ration cases, and virtually anything else that would burn. He assembled a huge pile near the landing pad and set it all on fire. The fire caught immediately and burned with such an intensity that even 75 yards away it was producing what Gatz called, *"incredible heat. It worked like a charm."* The heat literally created its own weather system that dried out the moisture above it and burned a hole in the clouds that was large enough for even the CH-53s and Chinooks to land. Ironically, Gatz remembers that the first aircraft into the zone was a UH-34, the smallest and oldest of the transport helicopters in use at the time. The aircraft was likely attached to HMM-362, the only Marine '34 squadron left in Vietnam, and operating at that time from the helicopter carrier USS Okinawa, LPH 3, that was part of Special Landing Force (SLF) Alpha. Although HMM-362 was stationed off the coast and a relatively long flight to the A Shau compared to the squadrons in Quang Tri and Phu Bai, its presence in the far reaches of Dewey Canyon exemplified the *"all in"* approach of the air assets engaged against the communists throughout I Corps. Another early arrival at the zone was Lt. Dave White, who was flying a CH-46 D model, with HMM-262. White had arrived in Quang Tri in January and was quickly on his way to flying more than 1,000 missions in a single 13-month tour. His first combat flights were in support of Dewey Canyon. White recalled that the helicopters hadn't been able to get into the fire base for days, and he was highly complimentary of Gatz's creativity in setting fire. Nonetheless, *"It was tight,"* White said, regarding the amount of room he had to maneuver while descending through the hole in the clouds. Ultimately, the wounded and dead were recovered, and supplies were brought in as long as the heat lasted.

VICTORY BETRAYED — Ronald Winter

Although fire was a friend due to the ingenuity of Major Gatz, it also had a bad side as was illustrated a day later at FSB Erskine where Battery D was established. The battery had been firing *"prep"* missions all night prior to infantry operations the following day, and the accumulated powder bags had not yet been disposed of, as noted earlier. As Col. Barnum recalled, a helicopter bearing a load of artillery ammunition came in to the LZ at the same time that some of the troops had built a small fire to heat some C-Rations. The down blast from the rotors spread the fire into some accumulated debris and from there it hit the powder bags. Despite efforts to extinguish the blaze, it leaped into a powder pit that blew with such intensity that it spread into nearby positions, one after the other, and literally destroyed the entire position. Barnum said the explosions could be seen from FSB Cunningham, but there was nothing anyone could do from that vantage point. When the fires died down, *"Echo Battery was sent over to clean things up,"* and provide the fire support that was initially tasked to Battery D. An investigation determined that the incident was accidental and not caused by either combat or negligence, Barnum said, but it nonetheless emphasized that, *"you had to be careful on a Fire Support Base."*

The assault on Fire Support Base Cunningham reinforced the need for additional infantry troops to provide security for the firebases while the battalions of the 9th were pursuing their objectives. To that end, the previously planned-for addition of extra security for the operation was put into place. On 20 February, Companies E, G, and the command group of Lieutenant Colonel James J. McMonagle's 2nd Battalion, 3rd Marines, took over the mission of providing security for Fire Support Bases Cunningham and Erskine, relieving 9th Marines Companies G and L, which joined their respective battalions in the move southward. Years later, now

170

VICTORY BETRAYED — Ronald Winter

Gen. (ret.) McMonagle remembered that while the security detail assignment was considered less dangerous than field operations— *"they called us the Palace Guard"*—it nonetheless was no walk in the park. *"We had been working with the South Vietnamese on pacification efforts,"* prior to relocating to Dewey Canyon, he said. Now, half the battalion was in the midst of a battle zone where being shot at by snipers was a common enough occurrence, but they also *"took regular incoming from the Russian 122mm guns."* In addition, life at the bases was no picnic, with water shortages considered part of a normal day. *"We were using water from banana stalks for shaving,"* McMonagle said. By the time Operation Dewey Canyon ended a month later, the 2nd Battalion, 3rd Marines suffered one Marine killed in action and several more wounded. The presence of the 3rd Marine detachment in the Dewey Canyon Area of Operations proved that there was no *"safe"* place for any of the units operating there. There were some *"amenities,"* however. Harvey Barnum recalled that a huge pot of *"Mulligan stew"* was constantly bubbling at the FSB and was available to supplement the C-ration diets the infantry units ate while on patrol. It was regularly fed by whatever foodstuffs could be scrounged from rations and resupply. Barnum noted that a regular contributor to the stewpot was Lieutenant General Richard G. Stilwell, commander of XXIV Corps. *"Gen. Stilwell would drop in regularly,"* Barnum said, *"and he'd bring us onions, and potatoes,"* and other additions to help keep the Marines fed. *"He even delivered the mail one time,"* Barnum recalled.

John Wilkes also remembered Gen. Stilwell taking an intense personal interest in the operation. The I Corps chain of command included a mixture of Marine and Army brass, with the 3rd Marine Amphibious Force, commanded at that time by Lt. Gen. Robert E. Cushman Jr., in overall command of I Corps, which included XXIV Corps, commanded by Lt. Gen. Richard Stilwell. He was in command of numerous Army and Marine units in northern I Corps, including the 3rd Marine Division, which included the Marines fighting in Operation Dewey Canyon. So, Gen. Stilwell had more than a passing interest in how the operation was progressing. He was personally involved.[81]

John Wilkes remembered the general stopping by the 155mm battery for a chat early in the operation. *"He came down to the battery and sat with me, and talked for over an hour,"* Wilkes remembers. *"He apologized for the 101st not being in on the operation,"* Wilkes said. Lt. Gen. Stilwell would later write a highly complimentary report on the 9th Marines in Operation Dewey Canyon and recommended the regiment for the Army Presidential Unit Citation, an extremely rare occurrence.

While issues of security and the progress of the operation were priorities in the days after the attack on Fire Support Base Cunningham, the battle continued for the infantry battalions that were moving out toward their objectives. And the NVA were waiting for them every step of the way. On 17 February, while advancing along the right flank, elements of the 2nd Battalion exchanged small arms and supporting fire with an enemy company in a daylong running battle. During the action Corporal James Johnson, a squad leader in Company E, was directed to seize an NVA bunker complex which had pinned down Marines of Company H. As the squad advanced toward the bunkers it came under fire from an enemy machine gun 20 meters to their front. Cpl. Johnson called for supporting arms fire from gunships overhead and marked the hostile position with bursts from his grenade launcher.

However, *"They couldn't see the bursts from the air,"* Johnson recalled, *"so I grabbed a couple of orange panels we used to mark LZs, and waved them at the pilots,"* from his position atop a bunker, fully exposed to the NVA. The air crews did see that signal and commenced gun runs on the position, as the NVA unleashed a barrage of small arms fire at Cpl. Johnson, who leaped to a position of relative safety. Johnson later noted that the panels were riddled with holes from NVA bullets that came ever so close but did not strike him. He brought his squad on line and assaulted the bunker complex, adjusting the air strikes on his own position because of his proximity to the enemy. After the air strikes ceased, the pilots informed him that his actions drove 15 enemy soldiers into an open area behind the complex and that these North Vietnamese were killed by the helicopter crews. Cpl. Johnson then led an assault against the bunkers where he was wounded in the hand by a grenade fragment. Disregarding his injury, he continued the advance, shouting words of encouragement to his men and directing their fire. Having sustained a second grenade fragment wound, this time in his leg, Johnson still advanced on an enemy bunker, where he threw a hand grenade through the aperture, razing the position and killing its three occupants. Deploying his men around the bunker, he directed a search of the area which revealed a complex of three more bunkers and two dead North Vietnamese soldiers. As he was preparing to rejoin the rest of his platoon, Johnson heard moaning sounds from outside the squad's defensive perimeter. Suspecting an enemy trap, he alerted his men, then went alone to investigate the source of the noise. He found one mortally wounded and one seriously wounded Marine from Company H, who had been injured in the previous engagement. Corporal Johnson rendered first aid to the casualty, saving the man's life. Rejoining his platoon, he refused medical attention until all other casualties had been treated and medically evacuated.[82]

Decades later, when asked what inspired him to jump out in the open, putting himself in imminent danger, Johnson put his mission into basic and understandable terms. *"There is no time for thought process in an ambush. A fraction of a second delay makes the difference between living or dying. Your reaction must be automatic. A conditioned reflex. Fortunately, or unfortunately depending on how you look at it, the men in the 9th Marines had a lot of experience due to continuous contact."* He also had a viable concern for the safety of his squad, he noted, adding, *"To me, it was very simple. I was a hunter and a killer. That's exactly what a Marine rifleman does in combat. I was there to find the enemy, close with the enemy, and kill the enemy.'*[83]

AUTHOR'S OBSERVATIONS

These Aren't Parade Ground Marines

A helicopter crewman who was aboard a CH-46 Sea Knight when it was shot down in the spring of 1969 related a tale of being *'in the bush'* for several days until ground forces could get him back to an extraction point. During that time the crewman was expected to draw upon the rudimentary infantry training he received after graduating from Marine boot camp and was an active member of the squad he was assigned to, not just excess baggage.

The unit fought several skirmishes with the North Vietnamese during those days as it worked its way back to base camp. And in those skirmishes, the true nature of the professional Marine emerged. The crewman related seeing, *"Sergeants, who would just snap their fingers, or nod in a general direction, and the Marines in his unit would know exactly what he wanted them to do. They would position themselves to best advantage, usually without a word being spoken."* Back at the LZ or FSB the NCOs would drill these concepts into the squad or platoon, regardless of whether they were seasoned veterans or new guys. *"Out in the bush it all came together, and it was something to witness, and experience."*

The late James L. Johnson, Navy Cross recipient for heroism during Operation Dewey Canyon, was one such Marine. Every time he was interviewed for **Victory Betrayed**, or just engaged in casual conversation, he would boil all of the concepts and rules down to the basics. Johnson lived by one simple code of conduct. *"I am here to find the enemy, close with the enemy, and kill the enemy."*

175

That, Johnson said on several occasions, is the true—and in his mind—only task assigned to a Marine infantryman. Everything that every Marine did or does is aimed in one direction, finding, closing with and killing the enemy. Everything else is superfluous.

THE PUSH TOWARD LAOS

"The jungle was so thick you couldn't see more than the man beside you."

Some of the heaviest fighting of the Da Krong campaign took place from 18 to 22 February, the majority occurring within the sector assigned to Lt. Col. George W. Smith's 1st Battalion. On the morning of 18 February, Company A encountered stiff opposition from an enemy platoon dug into camouflaged, reinforced bunkers on a heavily forested ridge line, five kilometers southeast of FSB Erskine. Armed with small arms and automatic weapons, the enemy *"appeared to want to hold their position at all cost."* Preceded by air and artillery strikes, Company A assaulted and overran the position, counting more than 30 NVA dead. The following morning, 19 February, Company C moved through Company A's lines and continued the attack against the heavily reinforced hilltop emplacement, killing an equal number of NVA. Friendly casualties resulting from the two actions were one killed and 14 wounded. Pressing the attack through the bunker complex, Company C again made contact during the late afternoon on 20 February, engaging a large enemy force supported by small arms, grenades, and machine gun fire. Two hours later, the Marine assault, assisted by fixed-wing air strikes with napalm drops within 50 meters of the point Marines, carried the position, killing 71 NVA. Equipment captured included two Russian-made 122mm field guns, and a five-ton, tracked prime mover. The two 122mm artillery pieces, the largest captured during the Vietnam War, subsequently were evacuated.

VICTORY BETRAYED — Ronald Winter

The task of hauling the guns out fell to George Allen, then a 1st Lieutenant, who was the rigging officer for the 3rd Shore Party Battalion at Vandegrift Combat Base. Allen was tasked with the Herculean responsibility of ensuring that the non-stop demand for supplies—food, water, ammunition for everything from infantrymen's rifles to the largest artillery pieces, and myriad other special needs—was met accurately and quickly.

Since virtually all of Dewey Canyon's resupply missions were carried out by helicopter, Allen's team of riggers engaged constantly in selecting the proper supplies, laying them out on huge cargo nets —with each net containing the specific supply requisition for specific Landing Zones, Fire Support Bases, or even units in the field. Then, at the proper time, they hooked those nets to the underbelly of cargo helicopters, ensuring that each helicopter took that load to the proper destination, and doing it all over again and again.

But after the intact Russian artillery pieces were captured, Allen was ordered to take a team out to the Laotian border to retrieve the big Russian guns that made life miserable for the Marines literally since Dewey Canyon kicked off a month earlier. It was Allen's job to dismantle the guns (which were far too big if left intact to be carried by any of the military helicopters) rigging the sections with netting, and calling in US Army, Sikorsky-built, CH-54 Skycrane helicopters, which were the only ones capable of carrying that load.

The Skycrane was designed with an ungainly look, similar to a Dragonfly insect, with a bulbous cockpit, legs extending outward from the mid-section and an exceptionally long tail section. The Skycrane could settle down over an entire container, such as the cargo section of a tractor-trailer, and had tremendous lift capabilities. But they also were scarce, as only 105 were ever built, and they were in high demand for heavy-lift requirements, such as moving heavy

178

artillery that were not self-propelled, or that were to be positioned on firebases for which there was no overland access.

Allen and his team arrived at the artillery positions not long after the last of the fighting that cleared the zone, and found the field guns intact, although the zone was strewn with the bodies of the gun crews. That was no surprise. What was surprising was that the guns crews were not North Vietnamese soldiers.

What Allen found was Caucasian soldiers, with blond hair and blue eyes, and Russian uniforms! In addition, among the Russian soldiers' belongings were firing tables, which contained the fire control information (FCI) under standard conditions, in addition to calculations to correct for unusual situations. Again, the existence of firing tables at an artillery position was not surprising. What was surprising was that these tables were written in Cyrillic! More than a half-century after being assigned that mission, and successfully 'hauling' the Russian artillery out of the zone, to be reassembled in somewhat safer surroundings, Allen noted that he had been accompanied that day by a photographer from a stateside news magazine.

The photographer took myriad photos, Allen remembers, but none ever surfaced back in the States. The existence of Russian soldiers involved in direct combat against American forces was declared to be Top Secret, Allen said, and remained that way for decades after the war ended. As General Westmoreland had stated nearly a year earlier, the Vietnam War would never be won militarily so long as America's politicians and bureaucrats continued to insist that it not be *"widened."* As the recovery of the Russian artillery, and discovery of the bodies of Russian combat troops showed, the war had already been widened. American troops were not only in danger as a result, but were denied the ability to respond appropriately, both to secure themselves, and to defeat an enemy that already was fighting against us. One of the field guns is on display at the Marine Corps Air-Ground Museum, Quantico, Virginia.

On the morning of 21 February, Lt. Col. Smith ordered Company A to send a platoon back to assist Company C in securing the artillery captured the previous day. The 3rd platoon was given the assignment. But on the way back to assist Company C, it ran into what 1st Lt. Wesley L. Fox called *"a massive force,"* and began taking casualties. Lt. Col. Smith ordered the rest of Company A into the fray. The 3rd platoon, with help from the rest of the company, was able to reach a relatively secure position. Company A continued the attack through Company C's forward lines, overrunning yet another enemy emplacement, killing another 17 NVA and seizing a two-and-one-half-ton truck and assorted artillery and anti-aircraft ammunition. Marine losses sustained in the two actions were five killed and 28 wounded in Company C, and one killed and two wounded in Company A.

On the morning of 22 February, Company A continued to reconnoiter the site of the previous day's contact, and then headed east off the ridge. According to Lieutenant Fox, companies A and C were moving toward Laos along one ridge line, while companies B and D were on a parallel course on another ridge line. About 1,000 meters from the battalion command post, near Lang Ha on the border, the 1st Platoon encountered an NVA squad in well-positioned bunkers. Under 2nd Lieutenant George M. Malone, Jr., the platoon quickly overran the position, killing seven while losing one Marine. What the Marines of Company A didn't know was that they had pushed past the main force of an NVA unit and had engaged with an outpost. *"At this point,"* observed Lt. Fox, *"it looked like that was all the resistance we had. Everything was quiet, so I radioed up to battalion to send the water details*

180

VICTORY BETRAYED — Ronald Winter

[from Headquarters and Service and C Companies] down to the creek. We were in bad need of water. The helicopters could not get in due to weather, and the battalion was low." A 20-man detail moved down and as they started to fill canteens, they came under enemy 60mm mortar and machine gun fire. *"We got the water detail out, but I could hear the mortars popping, as they left their tubes,"* Fox said. He reoriented his 1st Platoon toward the south and moved it forward. Pushing through triple-canopied jungle, that included banana groves, and underbrush so thick that it was easy to lose sight of the Marines around them, Lt. Malone's platoon ran up against a reinforced NVA company in a heavily fortified bunker complex. Behind them, on a high ridge line, the enemy was looking right down on the Marines and unleashed RPGs, machine guns, and mortars. While the dense foliage and heavy cloud cover made it impossible to bring in air support, or to accurately direct artillery fire, it also helped the Marines, Fox noted, as the triple canopy jungle *"made the NVA machine guns and mortars ineffective,"* by deflecting the bullets and causing the mortars to explode prematurely.

Fox moved the 3rd Platoon forward, and placed it on line with the 1st Platoon. Even with the addition of another platoon, the enemy resistance was strong, and the 2nd Platoon was then committed through the center of the two attacking platoons. At this point, Lt. Fox essentially had a full company on line in the assault, which normally would have meant about 200 Marines. However, recalling the battle nearly 5 decades later, Fox, by then a retired Colonel, said the Marine force numbered approximately 90 men. *"We were a month on duty (in Operation Dewey Canyon) with few replacements,"* Fox recalled, adding *"a basic rule of thumb, when assaulting a defended position, is that the attackers should outnumber defenders by a three-to-one ratio."* The Marines had nowhere near that number, and in fact were outnumbered by the NVA. Even though casualties were mounting, Lieutenant Fox found he could not use air and artillery support as the company was boxed in by a low ceiling, terrain, and vegetation. The company was so locked in combat that if he withdrew to use artillery, he would run the risk of incurring additional casualties. Momentum nevertheless had to be maintained. As the three platoons pressed the attack, the company command group took a direct mortar hit, killing or wounding everyone except the executive officer, First Lieutenant Lee R. Herron, who was given command of the 2nd Platoon. Lieutenant Fox, despite his wounds, continued to control the advance. *"As we got closer, we were in a heavy firefight,"* Fox said, *"and the jungle was so thick you couldn't see more than the man beside you."*

As he was maneuvering the troops and seeking an opening in the defenses, a sniper fired at him, barely missing. *"I was armed with a .45 pistol, but I saw the NVA up in the trees. So, I grabbed an M-16 from a dead Marine and took care of the sniper."* The forward momentum had all but stalled as the Marines pressed into stiff resistance, and Fox recalled wondering, *"What am I going to do?"* He couldn't disengage without abandoning the dead and wounded, so he was left only with one option, to put all platoons on line and overrun the NVA position. The sky was still overcast with a misty rain falling, and the jungle was so dense that he couldn't pinpoint NVA positions for the artillery. *"I was about to give the order to attack when the sky suddenly opened up,"* Fox said. *"Two OV-10 Broncos were on station and they knocked that sucker out,"* referring to the center of the NVA defense. *"We continued the assault, right through the NVA lines, ultimately linking up with Company D that had been ordered to join the battle. Company D was moving through the banana groves in front of Company A's position. They had gotten off on the wrong trail and came in behind the enemy position, and then walked into our front. At this time,"* Fox noted, *"I realized that we had already pushed through the entire position. Delta Company helped us mop up and carry up our dead and wounded."* Results included 105 NVA killed as confirmed by body count, and 25 automatic weapons captured. The dead, clad in new uniforms, included several officers, all of whom were highly decorated veterans of other campaigns. Marine casualties were 11 killed and 72 wounded, 54 of whom required evacuation. *"Thanks to the Lord for opening the sky, or we would have had a lot more casualties,"* Fox said. He was later awarded the Medal of Honor for his actions that day.

FOX, WESLEY L.

Rank and organization: Captain, U.S. Marine Corps, Company A, 1st Battalion, 9th Marines, 3d Marine Division. Place and date: Quang Tri Province, Republic of Vietnam, 22 February 1969. Entered service at: Leesburg, Va. Born: 30 September 1931, Herndon, Va.

Citation:

For conspicuous gallantry and intrepidity at the risk of his life above and beyond the call of duty while serving as commanding officer of Company A, in action against the enemy in the northern A Shau Valley. Capt. (then 1st Lt.) Fox's company came under intense fire from a large, well-concealed enemy force. Capt. Fox maneuvered to a position from which he could assess the situation and confer with his platoon leaders. As they departed to execute the plan he had devised, the enemy attacked and Capt. Fox was wounded along with all of the other members of the command group, except the executive officer. Capt. Fox continued to direct the activity of his company. Advancing through heavy enemy fire, he personally neutralized 1 enemy position and calmly ordered an assault against the hostile emplacements. He then moved through the hazardous area coordinating aircraft

support with the activities of his men. When his executive officer was mortally wounded, Capt. Fox reorganized the company and directed the fire of his men as they hurled grenades against the enemy and drove the hostile forces into retreat. Wounded again in the final assault, Capt. Fox refused medical attention, established a defensive posture, and supervised the preparation of casualties for medical evacuation. His indomitable courage, inspiring initiative, and unwavering devotion to duty in the face of grave personal danger inspired his Marines to such aggressive action that they overcame all enemy resistance and destroyed a large bunker complex. Capt. Fox's heroic actions reflect great credit upon himself and the Marine Corps and uphold the highest traditions of the U.S. Naval Service.[85]

As with Company G's fierce battle earlier in the month, the issue of bringing the dead and wounded to a suitable Landing Zone for helicopter evacuation brought its own challenges. But, as with Company G, the Marines of companies A and D made the arduous trek through the steep, sometimes rocky and always jungled terrain, carrying their dead and wounded with them, including Lt. George Malone, who had been wounded when the mortar hit the command position. Finally, they reached their objective, but *"it was midnight before everyone was off that ridge,"* Fox said. Company D was charged with destroying weapons captured from the NVA. But as occurred with Company G, the story didn't end there. During much of the afternoon on 22 February, Marine air crews braved enemy fire and flying conditions that should have grounded them to evacuate a total of 58 wounded Marines. Many of the Marine crewmen in those flights were decorated for their actions that day, including LCpl.

VICTORY BETRAYED — Ronald Winter

Douglas M. Braman, a crew chief on a CH-46 Super D helicopter who was awarded the Bronze Star (Single Mission) Air Medal for Heroism in Aerial Flight after crewing 8 separate missions into the LZ. Also decorated that day were corpsman Larry Sherer, and gunner Ed Oliver. Braman's citation noted that the flying conditions were hazardous with the aircraft flying at 200 feet above sea level due to the low ceiling, and NVA firing at the medevac flights both arriving at and leaving the LZ, where they were exposed to *"an intense volume of enemy automatic weapons and small arms fire."* But the remarkable aspect of Braman's heroics, considering how many medals were awarded during that fight, including the Medal of Honor awarded to Lt. Fox, and two Navy Crosses, was that Braman didn't receive it until more than a year later, due apparently to a bureaucratic snafu, after he had been released from active duty. It arrived in the mail and stayed under wraps at his home in Hebron, Connecticut and elsewhere for more than 3 decades, until a friend alerted the regional Marine infantry reserve regiment, and a special awards ceremony was held at the local veterans' post in September 2001. In a 150-year-old, former two-room schoolhouse, packed with veterans, family members, well-wishers, and the media, Braman finally received his medal in a fitting ceremony. But afterward, when asked by the media to describe the actions of that day, Braman responded that he didn't remember it as being *"any different than any other day,"* in that operation. The media carried that comment and friends agreed that it wasn't a matter of either bravado or false modesty, but rather a frank and honest comment on the conditions that marked what was a normal day for the Marines engaged in Operation Dewey Canyon. Simply put, acts of heroism were a daily occurrence in Dewey Canyon across the spectrum of infantry, artillery, air, and logistics units.

Braman's viewpoint on the mission is validated by at least one other crew member, who also was decorated for bravery, as were the rest of the crew members on the flight.

Corpsman Larry Sherer flew hundreds of medevac missions, including many on or over the Laotian border to extract Marine reconnaissance teams, or Army Special Operations units. He said the mission was so similar to others that, like Braman, he didn't know he had been decorated for bravery until the medal arrived at his home at least a year after the action.

However, Ed Oliver, flying as a gunner on the same aircraft as Sherer, had seen his share of hot LZs during medevac missions and remembers, *"It was raining and there were bodies everywhere. I have never seen that many KIA and WIA. I remember picking up this one Marine who had a poncho over him. I thought he was a KIA, and suddenly a hand came from under the poncho, and he pulled it back and said, 'Don't let me die!' That was one of the worst days of my life."* Oliver also remembers coming under *"heavy automatic weapons fire as we left the LZ."*

Due to Company A's daylong battle, the 1st Battalion reoriented its direction of search eastward, towards Hills 1044 and 1224 (Tam Boi). During the next four days, it moved along Route 548, just north of the border, encountering groups of enemy personnel and discovering several arms caches. The effort to take Tam Boi was assigned to 3rd Battalion, 9th Marines and it turned out to be as difficult as any during Operation Dewey Canyon. Warren Wiedhahn described it as, *"a fierce, fierce fight, with severe resistance,"* from the NVA. Advances by the battalion's companies were measured in yards, and sometimes even feet as they neared Hill 1224. Finally, at the end of a long day of fighting, Wiedhahn decided to call in airstrikes on the hill to give the Marines a better chance of advancing against the dug-in communists in the morning. As it turned out, Major Fred Gatz, who had conceived of lighting the fire at FSB Cunningham a few days earlier to give resupply and medevac helicopters an opportunity to land in the thick fog, was part of the assaulting force against Tam Boi. He was charged with calling in air support. However, Gatz found it difficult to link up with air assets that could divert to Tam Boi, due to heavy commitments elsewhere. Ultimately, as Wiedhahn recalled, he did find one aircraft, and in a turn of good fortune it happened to be a Boeing B-52H Stratofortress with a full load of unexpended bombs that had not been used on its primary target. Gatz worked out the coordinates of the bombing run as the word passed to the troops to pull back some 1,000 yards. That order was not exactly welcome among those who had spent the day taking that ground from the North Vietnamese—until they were told the reason behind the order. *"We pulled back to the other side of the mountain,"* Wiedhahn explained, and the B-52 unleashed its payload from somewhere in the vicinity of 30,000 feet above the battlefield. The NVA had no idea what was coming and suddenly a full load of bombs hit not only the top of Tam Boi, but the forward and reverse slopes as well. The next morning the Marines of the 3rd Battalion, 9th Marines renewed their assault, taking the ridge with *"relatively less resistance,"* as Wiedhahn explained it, in the process capturing a base camp dug into the mountain, as well as two Russian 122mm artillery pieces and considerable supplies. The B-52 had done its job, and *"an area that had been dense jungle the previous day was gone."*

The Arc Light had not only decimated the NVA positions, but took down trees along the reverse slope that made it impossible for them to retreat with their Russian-made artillery. The Marines set up a command post on high ground in the area occupied a day earlier by the NVA, but that wasn't the end of the fight. The NVA counterattacked that night from three directions simultaneously, and kept up the assault virtually the entire night, without success. Ultimately, the 3rd Battalion eliminated the NVA threat and took control of the massive underground complex, as well as the Russian 122mm field guns. In the end, *"We broke down the guns and hauled them out,"* Wiedhahn noted.[86]

AUTHOR'S OBSERVATIONS

Grinding It Out

When the weather cleared sufficiently for Phase Three of Operation Dewey Canyon to finally get going as originally intended, the NVA had moved significant numbers of troops into position to block the advance. Their job was to prevent the 9th Marines from achieving their objective—clearing the A Shau Valley of communists and preventing them from launching spring offensives against the civilian population of South Vietnam.

But in life, there is saying and there is doing. The communists may have *intended* to stop the Marines, but doing it was a different matter entirely. The communists set up blocking forces, ambushes, artillery, mortars and anything they could conceive of, but none of it worked. In retrospect, charting the Marine advance across the Area of Operations toward Base Area 611 is like watching a New York Giants football game—particularly in the seasons when the Giants win the championship.

The games, like the Marines' advance, may not be flashy, but by grinding it out on every play, combining an irresistible offense with an immovable defense, they just wear their opponents down. Of course, in football, there is always another play, another game, another year. And there the similarities end. In war, it is all or nothing, win or lose, no coming back for another play.

And from LZ Cunningham to the Ho Chi Minh Trail, it was the 9th Marines who dominated. They took everything the communists threw at them, tossed it aside, and just kept coming. The communists

190

must have felt like they were fighting Smokin' Joe Frazier. Hit the guy with your best shot and he laughs at you, then hits you back, harder.

It's no wonder, that when the 2nd Battalion crossed into Laos, the communists were terrified. They knew what their future held, and it would be short, and deadly.

WON'T YOU COME INTO MY PARLOR?

"What could they do, shave my head and send me to Vietnam?"

As the Marine battalions neared the Laotian border, concern over enemy artillery attacks, protection of the regiment's right flank, and potentially lucrative enemy targets generated plans and requests for the deployment of troops across the international boundary. After discussion at division and with XXIV Corps, Major General Davis forwarded a message to General Abrams at Military Assistance Command Vietnam (MACV) in Saigon requesting that the Special Operations Group (SOG) expand and redirect ground reconnaissance and exploitation operations, codenamed Prairie Fire, being carried out in nearby Laos, toward Base Area 611.

Reacting to the NVA artillery attack of 2 February on FSB Cunningham, Davis initially requested that the 9th Marines be permitted to enter Laos and destroy the threat. *"From the present position of the 9th Marines, a raid by a force of two battalions could be launched quickly and effectively to cut road No. 922 and moving rapidly back to the east, destroy artillery forces and other forces and installations which threaten us."* [87] Davis' request was shelved since the Rules of Engagement did not permit sending a large combat force into Laos to conduct a secondary search and destroy operation, which could possibly be viewed as an expansion of the war. The rules did permit United States and other Free World Forces to *"maneuver, while actually engaged and in contact with enemy forces, into Laos as necessary for the preservation of the force,"* and employ artillery and air strikes on threatening military targets. The rules also allowed commanders to take the *"necessary counteractions against VC/NVA forces in the exercise of self-defense and to defend their units against armed attacks with all means at their disposal."* These exceptions provided the 9th Marines with the justification the regiment needed. As Col. Barrow's troops moved further south, it became increasingly clear that the enemy was making extensive use of Route 922, either to reinforce or to withdraw his forces. *"In either case, interdiction of the road was clearly essential,"* noted Colonel Barrow. *"Efforts by B-52 arc light strikes, fixed-wing attacks, and unobserved artillery had been to no avail. He was continuing to use it. During the day the AOs were reporting fresh vehicle tracks, including tracked vehicles on the road, and as our forces moved further south, we could hear vehicles on the road. This was a pretty unacceptable situation, and it cried out for some sort of action to put a stop to it."* [88]

By 20 February, two companies, E and H, of Lieutenant Colonel Fox's 2nd Battalion had fought their way right up to the Laotian border, and more Marines were on the way, within a day's march. But having reached the border, US forces were required to stop at an invisible line in the jungle, peering down on Route 922 beyond, watching with increasing frustration as NVA convoys took their time moving armored vehicles, and trucks full of supplies, along the road, impervious to the massing US forces within rifle shot, to say nothing of artillery. As Captain David F. Winecoff later reported: *"The company, of course, was talking about let's get down on the road and do some ambushing. I don't think they really thought that they were going to let us go over into Laos, ... I knew if the military had their way we'd be over there in Laos and the company was all up for it .... With the Paris Peace Talks going on, I wasn't sure what route was going to be taken."* Winecoff reported the observations and fire missions, but from *"1,700 meters away it is difficult to zero in on movement."* The information provided by Winecoff's company, and intelligence gathered by SOG teams and 1st Radio Battalion intercepts, indicated that the enemy was evacuating its heavy artillery westward out of the reach of the 9th Marines. The

VICTORY BETRAYED — Ronald Winter

US Army's XXIV Corps commander, Lieutenant General Stilwell, revived Davis' initial request. In a message to Lieutenant General Cushman on 20 February, he recommended a limited raid into the heart of enemy Base Area 611 to a maximum depth of five kilometers along a 20-kilometer front. If, however, the proposal was *"beyond the realm of political acceptability,"* he suggested a lesser course of action which would involve the use of a Marine company as an extraction force if SOG reconnaissance teams encountered trouble. According to Stilwell, *"this would multiply the number of SOG RT teams which could be deployed simultaneously."* [89]

The mission of the Special Operations Group's Prairie Fire program provided for cross border reconnaissance operations into the panhandle of Laos using combined US/RVN forces to locate, interdict, and destroy enemy personnel and equipment on infiltration routes into South Vietnam. [90]

The SOG operations were independent of Operation Dewey Canyon, but not always independent of the Marine air crews supporting the operation. On March 1 a flight of CH-46 helicopters was launched to aid in the rescue of a SOG force that was pinned down approximately 5 miles inside Laos. The team—comprised of Army Special Forces troops and indigenous Laotian anti-communists—was surrounded and under heavy fire. One CH-46 from HMM-161 piloted by 1st Lt. John Robert "Bob" Odom and 1st Lt. Bo Honeycutt, flew into the zone and immediately came under heavy fire. Bullets ripped through the aircraft, which had a full team of reaction forces aboard. The aircraft lost electrical power to its communication and navigation systems, stability systems, one engine was disabled, and the flight controls were severely damaged. The aircraft turned toward FSB Cunningham, nearly 10 miles away, with Odom and Honeycutt working the controls together. Upon arriving at Cunningham there were other aircraft blocking the LZ, and since the pilots had no operational communications equipment, the air crews were forced to use smoke grenades, along with hand signals to alert ground personnel to their plight. Ultimately, the aircraft landed safely. All crew members except Odom received minor shrapnel wounds. The helicopter was airlifted back to Quang Tri and a few days after the mission, the squadron maintenance NCO approached Odom and Honeycutt with a metal bar in his hand. Odom recognized it as a central component in the flight control system, with a hole in it from an enemy bullet. As it was examined, the piece broke apart. Had that happened in flight, the aircraft would have crashed.

Back on 20 February, Cushman, in a message to General Abrams, passed on the suggested courses of action and noted that *"while recognizing the political implications of Gen Stilwell's proposals, ... balanced against the military value of this unique opportunity, I fully endorse both."* The matter of an incursion into Laos was now left up to General Abrams.

Events in the field, however, moved more rapidly. Company H, on the night of 20 February, again observed heavy truck traffic on Route 922. Winecoff reported the observations, and once again the company directed fire missions on the targets, but with unknown results. The following afternoon, Captain Winecoff received a hand-coded message, the result of several days of planning, from Colonel Barrow directing him to set up a company ambush along Route 922 that evening, with specific instructions to be back in South Vietnam no later than 0630 the next morning. *"Hotel Company,"* reported Barrow, *"was in the best position, really the only position to do it, and the job fell to them."* Winecoff immediately requested a 24-hour postponement because of the limited time available and the condition of his men, most of whom had been on patrol since early morning. Barrow denied his request. With no time to rehearse and little time to plan, Captain Winecoff decided to use only his 1st and 2nd platoons, as the men of the 3rd were exhausted after several tiring days of continuous patrol. At 1610, the company command group and the 1st Platoon, reinforced by mortar, forward observer, and machine gun teams, moved out for the 2nd Platoon's position at the bottom of the ridge, leaving the 3rd as security. Making good time over difficult terrain, they joined the 2nd Platoon a little over an hour later, and the 1st passed through the 2nd Platoon's position to establish the planned order of march. At 1800, after a meal and a 30-minute forward reconnaissance, the order arrived to execute, and Winecoff quickly briefed the company on ambush tactics, signals, and night movement. [91]

Shortly after dark, the company headed toward the road, 900 meters away. Staying off trails and using a creek bed and then a ridge line to minimize noise, the point element reached the small river which paralleled Route 922 at about 2030. Winecoff halted the column and sent his lead platoon commander and the chief scout— an experienced Marine sergeant, forward to find a route across the stream and to select an ambush site. As the company waited, it observed six trucks pass in front of its position; each stopping for a short period to *"recon by silence."* A tracked vehicle mounting a spotlight also passed. *"It was a very exciting moment for Hotel Company because the spotlight was scanning up and down the river and on the bluff, and it was playing over the lead elements of the company, but we were not spotted. Finally, it proceeded on down the road."* The two-man reconnaissance team returned around 2215, and after a quick brief, the company moved forward, crossing the river in column formation and then the road. About 35 meters beyond, Winecoff halted the company and set up a hasty linear ambush with the 1st Platoon on the right, and the

2nd on the left, and the command group in the center. Within minutes of moving into position, the Marines heard trucks approaching from the west. They passed the word to let the vehicles proceed through the ambush site, as the claymores and flank security were not yet in place. By 0100 in the morning of 21 February, the ambush was ready. With the men of Company H about 500 meters inside Laos, Colonel Barrow informed higher-ups of the move, *"thinking that even that much of a minor violation might in itself provide a little bit of assurance of approval. There was a little bit of opposition to what we were doing, and much discussion"* noted Barrow, *"and finally approval came through that, yes, we could do what we were going to do, but the implication clearly was, you had better make it work."* While the 9th Marines' staff obtained approval, Winecoff's men waited. The wait was not long. Less than ten minutes after setting up the ambush, a single NVA appeared, aimlessly walking along the road firing his AK47 rifle into the brush. Not wanting to *"bag one NVA soldier,"* Winecoff passed the word to let this *"dude"* walk through the killing zone.[92]

Forty minutes later, flank security detected a single truck approaching. Again, not wanting to destroy just one vehicle, Winecoff passed the order to let it through, instructing his forward listening post to visually check its contents. As it turned out, the truck carried a load of lumber. The next half hour was tense for Winecoff's men. Nothing moved, but voices could be heard 800 to 1,000 meters off to the right. *"I felt,"* Captain Winecoff noted, *"that sooner or later something was going to be coming along into the killing zone."* The company continued to wait. Meanwhile, a radio request came in from the battalion asking for a status report. They were *"afraid that we'd blown it,"* but Winecoff assured them otherwise. At 0230, the lights of eight trucks suddenly appeared off to the east. All positions were alerted. As the trucks moved closer, stopping now and then to *"recon by silence,"* the men of the ambush braced for action. Three of the vehicles had already entered the killing zone when the entire column stopped. Fearing that the enemy would detect his ambush, Winecoff detonated his claymore. With a loud roar and a boiling cloud of thick, black smoke, the mine disabled the second truck, killing its three passengers. As the smoke cleared, Winecoff could see that the explosion had also set the first truck afire and forced the third off the road. Small arms and automatic weapons fire poured into the vehicles from the flanks. *"Everybody had been waiting a long time and the excitement was keen."* Within seconds the forward observer alerted the artillery and rounds bracketed the company position.[93]

After several minutes of unrestricted fire, Winecoff gave the signal to move forward, making sure everything within the ambush site was destroyed. Once on the other side of the road, the company was given *"left face,"* and *"we proceeded in column right back in the same direction we came, crossing the river in the exact area, up the other side, and went about 500 to 600 meters up to a rally point where we hung 'till day-light."*

Later, the company rejoined the 3rd Platoon on the ridgeline where it was resupplied and the men given a rest. In addition to the three trucks destroyed, H Company counted eight NVA dead. Not a single Marine had been killed or wounded by enemy fire. First reports of the ambush to reach the 3rd Marine Division were sketchy and based largely on monitored 9th Marines radio traffic. Colonel Martin J. Sexton, 3rd Division Chief of Staff, immediately recommended that only XXIV Corps and III MAF be informed of the incident and that no report would be relayed to MACV until Brigadier General Frank E. Garretson had prepared a *"spot report in compliance with directives pertaining to rules of engagement."* On being informed of the ambush, Brigadier General George E. Dooley, III MAF Chief of Staff, was elated: *"Hit 'm hard! Good news—who knows where the border is anyway?"* [94] General Dooley may have been speaking off the cuff, but he gave voice to a physical reality on the ground that was ignored in Washington, D.C. and elsewhere.

As noted earlier, parts of eastern Laos had been annexed by the North Vietnamese communists in 1958. The district which included the transportation hub of Xepon, (or Tchepone), directly west of Khe Sanh, was physically taken by North Vietnamese forces who claimed it as recovered territory and raised the North Vietnamese flag over the district from that point onward. After a series of coups and counter-coups in the late 1950s and early 1960s left the Laotian government in shambles, a coalition government was formed in 1962. Although American, Russian and Chinese forces had ostensibly withdrawn from Laos that year in accordance with the international agreement, the North Vietnamese communist forces not only continued to use Laos as a staging and maneuvering platform without so much as a pause in activities, they expanded it greatly with each passing year, based on North Vietnam's claim that they were actually operating in their own country.[95] Thus, the exact location of the border was a matter of who was talking. US diplomats and politicians saw it as a definitive line using maps drawn decades earlier, while the North Vietnamese saw it as existing much further to the west. Since they held the territory, their point of view ruled on the ground, regardless of what was decided in embassies thousands of miles away, and it was the communist point of view that physically affected US forces operating all along the 'border.'

About mid-afternoon on 22 February, a reply to Stilwell's and Cushman's messages of 20 February arrived at III MAF. Responding to their proposals, General Abrams stated emphatically that *"all operations in connection with Base Area 611 will be with SOG forces,"* and that close coordination between Marine units in South Vietnam and

SOG teams in Laos was authorized. Although an apparent conflict existed between the action of Company H, 2nd Battalion, 9th Marines, and General Abrams' directive, Garretson solved it in his report by referring to the appropriate rules of engagement permitting a local commander to exercise the right of self-defense. However, larger questions remained. With all three battalions on or just north of the border, and substantial enemy installations and lines of communication directly ahead, what future direction was Operation Dewey Canyon to take? Was the international boundary to remain a permanent barrier to the 9th Marines?[96]

While the ambush itself was dramatic and successful, its real value, according to Colonel Barrow, lay in the leverage it provided to request a continuation of such operations in Laos. *"Therefore, the next day I sent a message to higher headquarters stating why we had done what we had done, reiterating the successes achieved, and then my final paragraph made an urgent request for authority to maneuver into Laos ... . This generally was about a 2,000-meter extension and included all of Route 922."* Again, he stated that his request was based upon the *"immediate and constant"* enemy threat to his troops and on intelligence, which continued to place enemy troops and equipment concentrations in the area. And, noted Barrow, *"I put a final comment on my message, which said, quote, 'put another way, my forces should not be here if ground interdiction of Route 922 not authorized.'"* [97]

Lieutenant General Stilwell also would not give up. Adopting Barrow's recommendations, he requested authority from MACV for *"a selected advance south to the east-west gridline—a distance not exceeding two kilometers from the border at any point."* Faced with a fait accompli, General Abrams finally approved Stilwell's request on 24 February, but placed restrictions on all public discussion of the Laotian incursion, fearing possible adverse effects on international policy.

Knowledge of the operation was also to be limited. The American ambassador in Laos, William H. Sullivan, for example, was not informed until the operation was well underway, as was Laotian Prime Minister Souvanna Phouma, who when informed, *"expressed understanding of the action and said the essential element was to keep the matter secret,"* but hoped it would be short.[98]

Within hours of General Abrams' approval, Company H, 2nd Battalion, 9th Marines was again instructed to *"move back down onto the bloomin' Route 922."* According to Captain Winecoff, the men's *"morale zoomed way down because the company was extremely tired, [and] we were afraid that we were going to have to go off and leave our supplies .... This included half a pallet of 60mm mortar ammunition, quite a few C-rations, and of course not the beer, we consumed that."* [99]

Nonetheless, the 2nd Battalion moved across the border into Laos, heading east on the Ho Chi Minh Trail, and began a solid week of overrunning communist positions, destroying equipment and facilities, and chasing communist units, generally into the guns of 1st and 3rd just across the border in South Vietnam. *"We went in and went west to Highway 922,"* recalled Jay Standish, *"then went east for several days. We had several firefights, and captured equipment including artillery. The NVA never expected it,"* he added. *"They were caught by surprise. They were in a full rout, a panic."*

The plan was for Company H, followed by Companies E and F, to move into Laos, and then drive eastward along Route 922, forcing enemy troops into the waiting sights of the 1st and 3rd Battalions. In addition, intelligence indicated that the NVA were desperately trying to evacuate their remaining artillery pieces in the face of the other two battalions' push southward. In essence, the direction of the operation was now toward removing the enemy threat to the regiment's right flank. Once again on the road, Company H, after a six-hour night march, set up another hasty ambush, and at 1100 on 24 February, engaged six unsuspecting NVA soldiers, killing four. Moving eastward the following day, another 10 were engaged, resulting in eight killed, one 122mm field gun and two 40mm antiaircraft guns captured. Marine losses were two dead and seven wounded. Later the same day, an estimated 15 enemy troops in fortified bunkers and fighting holes ambushed a company patrol. Reinforced, the patrol pushed through the enemy position, killing two and capturing a second 122mm gun. Marine casualties were three killed and five wounded. Among those who gave their lives was Corporal William D. Morgan, who in a daring dash, directed enemy fire away from two wounded companions, assisting in their rescue. For this action, he was posthumously awarded the Medal of Honor.

MORGAN, WILLIAM D.

Rank and organization: Corporal, U.S. Marine Corps. Company H, 2d Battalion, 9th Marines, 3d Marine Division. Place and Date: Quang Tri Province, Republic of Vietnam, 25 February 1969. Entered service at: Pittsburgh, Pa. Born: 17 September 1947, Pittsburgh, Pa.

Citation:

For conspicuous gallantry and intrepidity at the risk of his life above and beyond the call of duty while serving as a squad leader with Company H, in operations against the enemy. While participating in Operation DEWEY CANYON southeast of Vandegrift Combat Base, 1 of the squads of Cpl. Morgan's platoon was temporarily pinned down and sustained several casualties while attacking a North Vietnamese Army force occupying a heavily

---

fortified bunker complex. Observing that 2 of the wounded Marines had fallen in a position dangerously exposed to the enemy fire and that all attempts to evacuate them were halted by a heavy volume of automatic weapons fire and rocket-propelled grenades, Cpl. Morgan unhesitatingly maneuvered through the dense jungle undergrowth to a road that passed in front of a hostile emplacement which was the principal source of enemy fire. Fully aware of the possible consequences of his valiant action but thinking only of the welfare of his injured companions, Cpl. Morgan shouted words of encouragement to them as he initiated an aggressive assault against the hostile bunker. While charging across the open road, he was clearly visible to the hostile soldiers who turned their fire in his direction and mortally wounded him, but his diversionary tactic enabled the remainder of his squad to retrieve their casualties and overrun the North Vietnamese Army position. His heroic and determined actions saved the lives of 2 fellow Marines and were instrumental in the subsequent defeat of the enemy. Cpl. Morgan's indomitable courage, inspiring initiative and selfless devotion to duty upheld the highest traditions of the Marine Corps and of the U.S. Naval Services. He gallantly gave his life for his country.[100]

Company H and the battalion *"jump"* or field command group, continued to move eastward, flanked by Companies E and F, *"to have a force in position to launch a flank attack quickly were we hit from the rear (west)."* Progress was rapid, too rapid for some: *"I felt that if we had been moving slower and had more time to check things out, we probably would have found a heck of a lot more equipment than we did,"* noted Captain Winecoff.[101]

VICTORY BETRAYED — Ronald Winter

James Johnson fought the NVA alongside his brother Marines in Company E. *"Inside of Laos, we moved non-stop, it seemed, during the daylight hours into the twilight hours. Exhaustion was a big problem at this point of the operation. At nighttime, after humping all day and then digging in for the night, the S.O.P. was two hours on, two hours off. Imagine the strain of your mind and body. As always, walking point is the most exhausting thing you can do."* In addition to clashing with numerous NVA units, elements of the 2nd Battalion captured over 20 tons of foodstuffs, and thousands of rounds of ammunition, while killing 48 enemy soldiers. As the troops moved eastward back toward the Vietnam border, they found bunkers, fighting positions, and weapons caches, many left behind with no effort—or time—to conceal them.

However, a major issue evolved the longer 2nd Battalion stayed in Laos, because the battalion had crossed the border with limited rations and was running out of food. Due to the Rules of Engagement, helicopter crews were not allowed to resupply the infantry in Laos even though they were completely out of rations according to Jay Standish. *"The troops were starving,"* adding that he led a patrol out from the main body for *"only about 100 yards, but men were falling down due to starvation. I knew we couldn't patrol in that condition, so we returned."* The Marines had successfully overrun several NVA positions, but on the fourth day they came upon a well-defended NVA complex and the enemy put up stiff resistance, requiring an all-out assault to overcome them. The Marines discovered the NVA had been guarding a supply depot laden with food as well as other materials. *"There were 50kg bags of rice all over the place,"* Standish recalled, *"as well as cans of powdered nuoc mam,"* a form of dehydrated decomposed fish that was high in protein but smelled like nothing most of the Marines had ever encountered.

James Johnson recalls that fight as well, and the relief it brought to the Marines. *"The rice, as I remember, was found along the river, back inside of Laos. It was in sacks. For some reason, I want to say there were over two hundred bags of rice."* The issue of how to turn raw rice into food was solved with help from ARVN personnel who accompanied the Marines. *"We had Kit Carson scouts with us, and they showed us how to combine the nuoc mam and rice with water in C-ration cans to make meals,"* Standish said. The combination gave the Marines the carbohydrates and proteins they desperately needed to regain their strength and continue the mission. The irony of the Marines' plight was that resupply, always questionable in Dewey Canyon due to the weather, in this case would have been far more manageable. *"The weather was actually fairly nice on the Ho Chi Minh Trail,"* Standish said, *"but resupply was not possible due to the Rules of Engagement."*

In addition to scrounging food from captured enemy caches, the unavailability of helicopters for medevac and other matters also caused another set of problems. As James Johnson recalled it, *"In the heat of battle, you continue to fight until the enemy is either dead or you are. Other warriors may fall around you, but you cannot stop. You must continue to fight. After the engagement has ended, then you look around and reality sets in. Even if you are wounded, you are still better off than those lying there dead. To me, it was not the firefights or mortar or artillery attacks that had the big impact emotionally on the men. It was carrying our dead and wounded for days at a time that had the lasting memory effect on them. Because of the weather and our location, helicopters could not come pick the bodies up after we had engaged with the enemy. You have probably seen animals who have been killed with their front and back legs tied together, hanging from a pole. That is how sometimes you transport, until you can get to an area and get the dead wrapped in a poncho. The corpsman tries to keep the wounded medicated as best as he can."* The dead and the wounded who could not walk presented another set of challenges for the rest of the battalion. *"The dead and wounded*

VICTORY BETRAYED — Ronald Winter

are normally placed in the middle of a column because that is the weakest point of movement," Johnson said. The inability to medevac the wounded was both a physical and mental challenge for their fellow Marines. *"I saw a lot of guys wounded so bad, I am sure they wished they had died. I know I would have,"* Johnson said. In addition to the strain of carrying the badly wounded Marines, there were other issues with the dead Marines. *"The dead smell a lot, depending on how long it takes to get them to an area where they can be medevaced out,"* Johnson said. *"The smell of the dead will stay with you forever. Blood leaks from the ponchos, you can follow the trail if you're behind it. Then Rigor Mortis sets in, which is really a bitch. It normally sets in within six hours. Carrying the dead and wounded is different for everyone. I would always shut it out of my mind. It's called compartmentalization. Others would be affected very strongly by it. All that said, it is an experience all real warriors never forget. One minute the guy is next to you alive, next minute he is dead. That is why I learned to never get close to anyone."*

Absent the most basic forms of support, the Marines of 2nd Battalion created their own support, or took it from the enemy that was opposing them. The opportunity to refresh their own supplies, which for all practical purposes had run out, was made to order for a military force that literally was living off the land. Once rejuvenated, the 2nd Battalion continued its march eastward, overrunning communist positions and making the point in no small way that they were the dominant force in the theater. By 1 March, the three companies were within 1,000 meters of the South Vietnamese border, having covered over 5,000 meters in five days. They continued toward the border and crossing it, found a Lance Corporal holding a makeshift sign, stating *"Welcome to VN."*

Meanwhile, Harvey Barnum's Battery E was now atop Tiger Mountain in Firebase Turnage, having relocated to that position on 28 February, and was providing artillery support for the continuing operations on the edge of the A Shau Valley. Barnum recalls the Marines of 2nd Battalion returning to Vietnam with an intense level of pride in their actions.[102] Jay Standish recalled seeing the sign as he crossed what was considered to be the border since there were no other markers to provide its exact location. And the pride was evident to all who saw 2nd Battalion return from the incursion into Laos. *"We believed we had changed the course of the entire war,"* Standish recalled.[103]

Two days later, 2nd Battalion was heli-lifted to Vandegrift Combat Base. The battalion, while in Laos, sustained eight killed and 33 wounded, 24 of whom required evacuation. In keeping with the politics that defined the Vietnam War, all the dead from the Laos incursion were officially reported to have been killed *"near Quang Tri Province, South Vietnam."* No reference was made to Laos for political reasons. Even the citation awarded posthumously to Corporal William D. Morgan said he fought and died in Quang Tri, not Laos. The significance of these actions was more apparent later in the war, but for the moment there were more urgent matters at hand. When the 2nd Battalion arrived back at Vandegrift Combat Base, the first order of business was to feed the Marines who had spent the better part of a week at starvation levels. The cooks at the base had been alerted to their impending arrival and prepared accordingly. In the officer's mess Jay Standish said he set the tone by *"eating 14 steaks and drinking a six-pack of beer."* [104] With that, the 2nd Battalion's participation in Operation Dewey Canyon officially ended.

But the other battalions had not been idle while the 2nd Battalion was raiding the Ho Chi Minh Trail. On the left flank of the regiment's area of operations, although encountering lighter opposition, Lieutenant Colonel Laine's 3rd Battalion gained substantial results. Attacking generally down the trace of Route 922 within South

Vietnam, elements of the battalion uncovered numerous enemy facilities containing tons of supplies and equipment. On 18 February, Company L located an NVA cemetery containing 185 bodies, most of whom had been buried in June 1968. On 21 February, Company M found a well-camouflaged maintenance installation, complete with six repair pits, a bulldozer, a front-end loader, several disassembled engines, and more than three hundred 50-gallon fuel drums. Pushing southward, the battalion, after securing Hill 1228 (Tiger Mountain), began a detailed search of the Tam Boi mountain complex, discovering on 23 February two spiked 122mm field guns, along with a prime mover and assorted artillery, mortar, and small arms ammunition.[105] Also at Tam Boi the Marines discovered a huge headquarters and administrative complex that comprised 11 major tunnels carved into solid rock and housing extensive repair shops, storage rooms and a hospital. These facilities could withstand direct hits from artillery and aerial bombs. The tunnels at Tam Boi revealed sophisticated engineering abilities, as they were 150 to 250 meters long, cross-connected. The *"hospital was abandoned very rapidly, leaving one patient on the operating table to die."* All were capable of withstanding direct hits from air and artillery attacks.[106]

This was familiar territory to many Marines fighting in Dewey Canyon, including the air crews. Joseph Snyder, then a 1st Lieutenant flying as a section leader with 8 CH-46 Super D helicopters, had what was at least an unsettling experience there on 18 February, just as the cleanup on FSB Cunningham was in full swing. The CH-46s had been dispatched on a rescue mission to support an Army SOG team that was surrounded by the NVA. The Army helicopter, that had landed the team on the top of Tiger Mountain, was shot down, killing the pilots and crew—although the team escaped into the bush and was under heavy fire by an enemy force of unknown size. But the helicopter was sitting in the zone with its rotor blades still turning, and no one to fly it out or shut it down, providing a major obstacle to the quick reaction team that was dispatched to help. Marine Huey gunships were providing covering fire for the Special Forces team to keep it from being overrun. The job of the quick reaction force was to augment the Special Forces team and wipe out the enemy. Snyder recalled that as the flight approached the mountain, North Vietnamese gunners opened fire on the lead aircraft *"which took a direct hit in the cockpit and waved off. By this time in the war the NVA had figured out that if you wanted to bring a helicopter down, just kill the pilots."* The NVA troops then turned their attention to Snyder's aircraft hitting the cockpit, wounding the copilot and sending a round through the cuff of Snyder's flight suit, although he was unscathed. However, the bullets also disabled the aircraft hydraulic system, which is a fatal blow to the flight controls. Having no control, and unable to set down in the zone due to the disabled Huey, Snyder autorotated to the valley floor. A chase helicopter immediately followed him to the deck and the crew was successful in evacuating the Marines, taking the helicopter's .50 caliber machine guns and ammo with them. Unfortunately, as one of the helicopter gunners placed his .50 caliber machine gun on the deck of the chase helicopter, it discharged one round. Crew members flying as gunners were required to clear the chambers of live rounds before the guns are taken out of the helicopter, which obviously didn't happen on that flight. The round went through the deck of the chase helicopter, the pilot thought they were taking fire, and immediately took off, leaving Snyder on the valley floor, alone. It had been his job as the aircraft commander for the downed helicopter to ensure that everyone aboard was safely on the chase aircraft, thus he was still outside when the incident occurred. *"There I was,"* Snyder said, recalling the incident nearly five decades later, *"alone in bad guys' territory, with only my .38 caliber pistol and my rescue radio. Thank God for the radio. I called out a Mayday, hoping I would be heard. After a time, my wingman realized I was not on board, and returned to pick me up. I don't know how long I was on the ground, but it felt like eternity."* Snyder was safely extracted as the mission continued, but Tiger Mountain was squarely in the sights of the advancing Marines and would be revisited in a very short time.

Although the monsoon clouds had made helicopter resupply and medevac activity difficult during this period it did not halt them altogether. The pilots and air crews continued to bring as much food, water and ammo to the advancing infantry as they could, and to take out the medevacs. At times this required a level of inventiveness that simply was not taught, but much like the ingenuity shown by their counterparts on the ground, had to be developed on the scene. For example, there is an adage in Marine aviation that, *"Helicopters don't fly. They beat the air into submission."* That may have been intended as a joking reference to the sharp slap or pounding rhythm of helicopter blades as they made their way from one LZ to another. But during a flight on 23 February one pilot from HMM-161 literally made it come true. Major James S. Loop, who had been flying in the operation since the beginning, was resupplying beleaguered ground units, in this case 1st Battalion who were locked in heavy combat with the NVA and very much in need of ammo, water and other supplies. As usual, the flights were hazardous due both to enemy fire and the fact that the often small LZs were socked in by dense monsoon clouds. While Major Loop had already completed missions in the area under heavy fire, he received a call in the midst of the 'routine' flights for an emergency medevac for seven wounded Marines in the same area of the Da Krong valley. When he got to the vicinity of the zone where the wounded were awaiting evacuation, Loop lost visual contact with a flight of UH-1E 'Huey' gunships that had accompanied him. Nonetheless, he continued his efforts to locate the zone, despite enemy bullets directed at his aircraft and mortars hitting the LZ. A statement from 1st Lt. John Shavce who was flying one of the accompanying gunships that day notes that the cloud layer began at approximately 2500 feet, some 300 feet below the LZ. *"Their position was practically on the Laotian border,"* Lt. Shavce said. The only clearing, he noted, was over enemy positions to the southeast of the zone. Lt. Shavce assisted Maj. Loop by radio guidance until Loop could no longer see Shavce's aircraft through the clouds, and from there was on his own. Shavce and other gunships began a series of attacks on the enemy positions until they were out of ammo, and then continued to make runs to intimidate the NVA and keep their heads down.[107]

Years after the mission, Loop, by then a retired Lt. Col., remembered entering the eerie world of clouds, somewhere above the zone, with no means to get a visual reference. He was maneuvering using instruments that could tell him his altitude, both above sea level and the ground below him, but couldn't tell him what was in front or alongside his aircraft. *"Then I saw a tree,"* Loop recalled. Using the downdraft from his rotor blades to part the clouds and give him partial visibility, Loop maneuvered closer to the mountain. *"I would move in as close as I could safely, see the treetops, then lift up and move in again. Essentially, I 'walked' the aircraft up the side of the mountain, using the treetops as reference points. Meanwhile, we were communicating with the troops on the ground, and they were able to guide us to a spot over their zone. Even after we air taxied from tree to tree, we still had to descend into a very small opening, with trees all around us,"* he added. Finally, Loop was over the zone and carefully descended.

As if the flying conditions weren't bad enough, the NVA had

VICTORY BETRAYED — Ronald Winter

the zone zeroed in and had been dropping mortars into it for some time previously, hence the emergency medevacs. The condition of the wounded necessitated very careful handling, and the threat of incoming rounds, coupled with stretcher bearers and walking wounded making their way across the LZ in near zero visibility, considerably extended the amount of time the aircraft had to remain in the zone. During the time in the LZ, Lt. Shavce informed Loop that the gunships had expended all their rockets and machine gun ammo, and the zone was vulnerable to enemy fire. *"But he (Maj. Loop) decided to remain in the LZ until all the medevacs were aboard, despite the high threat of mortars, which had already hit the LZ itself, and although he was at 'bingo' fuel."* Loop's aircraft was in constant danger and he was aware of the increased vulnerability of his position, but still he remained on the ground as the wounded came aboard. Lt. Shavce's report states that Loop remained on the ground for a full five minutes, in a war where most landings were executed in a matter of seconds, and even a half-minute on the ground in a hot zone was considered an eternity. Ultimately, the wounded were safely aboard, and Loop began the reverse process of lifting out of the tight zone. Once above the cloud cover, he made a beeline for Vandegrift Combat Base where the wounded could be treated or transferred to higher level medical facilities. When interviewed in 2014 about his actions that day, Loop said simply, *"The credit goes to the crews. They made it happen."*[108] Nonetheless, Loop was awarded the Silver Star *"For conspicuous gallantry and intrepidity in action ..."* for his efforts that day.[109]

By late February the 9th Marines' objectives were falling one after the other, even while the 2nd Battalion was still in Laos. On 27 February, while searching the slopes of Hill 1044, Company D, 1st Battalion found one of the largest enemy weapons and munitions caches of the war. *"I was walking along the side of a road,"* Gunnery

Sergeant Russell A. Latona reported, *"and there was a bomb crater there and sticking out of the bomb crater I saw the footpod of a mortar bipod."* Alerting the company, he ordered several men to start digging. *"They dug down about four or five inches and they found boards. They lifted up the boards and they started digging a hole and this is when we found several weapons."* A further check of nearby bunkers and bomb craters revealed that the company had moved into the midst of an NVA supply depot, a storehouse which would eventually yield 629 rifles, 108 crew-served weapons (60 machine guns, 14 mortars, 15 recoilless rifles, and 19 antiaircraft guns), and well over 100 tons of munitions. The next two days were spent inventorying and then destroying the cache.[110]

While the assault on Tam Boi was progressing, elements of the 3rd Battalion also successfully secured Tiger Mountain. On 28 February E Battery, 2nd Battalion, 12th Marines moved to the top, and established FSB Turnage, named after a former 3rd Marine Division commander, General Allen H. Turnage. The fire support base, used the year before by the 1st Cavalry Division, was opened primarily to provide balanced artillery support for further operations of the 3rd Battalion in the northwest corner of Thua Thien Province. E Battery now could fire directly down on the Ho Chi Minh Trail.[111]

FSB Turnage also provided a stage for the artillerymen of 2nd Battalion, 12th Marines to put an exclamation point on their efforts during the previous two months. By the end of Operation Dewey Canyon more than 130,000 artillery rounds were expended. But a milestone was reached in late February as the battalion was nearing the 100,000th round fired. That honor went to E Battery, and Capt. Barnum arranged for an engraved shell cannister to be presented to Major Gen. Davis. Davis arrived at FSB Turnage as previously arranged, the shot was fired, and the cannister was presented to the general. But decades later, when Barnum, now a retired Colonel, was asked if there was a specific fire mission for that particular shell, he laughed and said, *"No."* When further questioned as to where the shot fell, Barnum said he pointed the gun in the general direction of communist positions in Laos and let loose. Although it probably could be considered Harassment and Interdiction (H&I) fire, when asked if the shot might have constituted a violation of the Rules of Engagement, Col. Barnum noted that he was in one of the most isolated sections of Vietnam, had been in constant combat with communist forces for nearly two months, and now was atop the most remote fire base in the theater, literally astride the border and looking right at the Ho Chi Minh Trail. *"I figured, what could they do,"* Barnum mused, *"shave my head and send me to Vietnam?"* [112]

While the 9th Marines enjoyed many successes, the 2nd Battalion also experienced two critical and persistent problems during the month-long push southward: resupply of units in the field and casualty replacement. Early in the operation it was found that resupplying rifle companies without halting their forward progress or pinpointing their positions was impossible. To make matters worse, once a company was ready to continue its advance after being resupplied, a squad or platoon often had to remain behind to secure transport nets, water containers, and other items until retrieved. This not only reduced company strength, but unnecessarily exposed the smaller unit to attack. An effort was made to improve this situation through the use of a Helicopter Emergency Lift Pack, designed and fabricated by the 3rd Shore Party Battalion. C-rations, ammunition, and other items were placed on wood pallets or bundled in discarded canvas, slung on inexpensive loop-type wire cables, and lifted into the field. Marines were then able to obtain their supplies, dispose of the packaging, and continue the advance with little or no delay. Initially included among the items of the Emergency Lift Pack were 5-gallon plastic water bottles, which did not supply the need of Marines in the field, and were subject to leakage. Instead of increasing the number of containers, 155mm, 175mm, and 8-inch artillery canisters, each capable of holding approximately 13 gallons of water were substituted and proved highly successful.[113]

In addition to often being short on supplies, several units sustained moderately high casualties, and, as a result, lost some effectiveness in the movement southward. Although anticipated in early planning, the 9th Marines, because of transportation problems due mostly to weather, often shifted personnel already in the field as needed. This tactic was successful in the short run, but in most cases, units had to operate for several days below the desired strength level before receiving new personnel. Replacements did get in, but the frequency was directly related to the weather and the flying conditions for the helicopters. One such replacement was Lance Corporal Marco Polo Smigliani, an Italian immigrant who joined Lt. Wesley Fox's Company A early in the operation. As a further indication of the danger faced by everyone in the Dewey Canyon area of operation, Smigliani was wounded on his first patrol. He recalls being hit in the back with shrapnel, possibly from an RPG. Whatever the immediate cause, he was slated to be medevaced out nearly as soon as he arrived but convinced the corpsman that he could stay in the field. Like virtually every other Marine in the operation, Smigliani remembers interminable *"humping"* and other Marines passing out from hunger and exhaustion. That facet of the operation prompted Smigliani to send a letter to his Drill Instructor from boot camp, thanking him for the physical training he had received. Smigliani was wounded a second time on 4 March while on patrol, and then a third and fourth time as he was leaving FSB Cunningham under fire.

AUTHOR'S OBSERVATIONS

Won't You Come into My Parlor?

To fully appreciate how the Marines who ambushed the NVA on the Ho Chi Minh Trail must have felt about their action, we have to appreciate the position the politicians and bureaucrats had put us in for the previous 7 years. Simply put, America's military was not allowed to use its best tactics, which pretty much made the overall strategy of defeating the communists and keeping South Vietnam free, moot. For all of that time, American forces were forced to sit on the South Vietnam side of the border and allow the communists to pick the time and place where we would fight.

I remember asking a warrant officer to whom I reported, after several 'initial assaults' into the DMZ and the Laotian border areas (there should have been only one of each, otherwise it isn't 'initial,' it's redundant) why we weren't allowed to just cross these invisible lines and take the battle to the enemy. He told me, and this was in the late summer of 1968, months before Dewey Canyon, that we were supposed to be a *"thorn in the side"* of the communists until the South could take over its own defense. Mind you, this was coming from a career Marine who had fought on Iwo Jima in WWII, was there for the Korean War and now was adding a third set of foreign war service ribbons to his already impressive decorations.

I remember being stunned, and thinking, *"Since when is it the objective of the United States Marine Corps to be a thorn in anyone's side?"*

So when the order was given to the 2nd Battalion, 9th Marines to go into Laos and kick some ass, you can bet those Marines were more than anxious to do just that. For the Star Trek fans who are reading this, remember in The Search For Spock, when Capt. Kirk is fighting Christopher Lloyd's Klingon character, who has just killed Kirk's son, and the Klingon is dangling over a volcanic lake of lava? Kirk offers to help him but the Klingon keeps fighting, so Kirk kicks him repeatedly in the face growling, *"I ... have ... had ... enough ... of ... you!"* And the Klingon finally falls into a lake of fire! And if you watched it in a theater people were cheering?

Yeah, it was a lot like that.

AUTHOR'S OBSERVATIONS

Breaking Their Stuff

The impact of two months of destruction on the NVA's ability to fight—in the midst of Operation Dewey Canyon and in their planned future operations—can't be overstated. In short, the Marines literally took the NVA out of the game for the foreseeable future, at least in that area of South Vietnam.

The vast quantities of foodstuffs, weapons, and ammunition were significant in their own right. But think of the facilities that were destroyed as well. Tam Boi was a prime example. While there were numerous other camouflaged sites that served as refuges, vehicle storage, and maintenance facilities, and they too gave up vast quantities of war materiel, there literally was nothing like Tam Boi.

Tam Boi was carved out of solid rock, and had massive tunnels running through it like a honeycomb. It housed troops, repair facilities, a hospital, administrative facilities and it was virtually impervious to anything but an infantry assault. Tam Boi could equip, house, feed, and heal hundreds of enemy troops, all hidden from view and impervious to air strikes and artillery.

In the end, it was the 3rd Battalion, 9th Marines that overran Tam Boi. But by all accounts, there would have been far more US casualties if Major Fred Gatz, the air liaison officer attached to the battalion, had not been able to rustle up a B-52 bomber to help out.

When tons of bombs rained down on Tam Boi's defenders in the dark of night, as the Marines were poised to make a final push in the morning, the defenses were shattered, many of the defenders killed, and the keys to the castle left lying on the ground, figuratively speaking. That Tam Boi was of major importance to the communists was evidenced by their repeated, albeit unsuccessful, counter-attacks.

In addition to the facilities and supplies captured in Operation Dewey Canyon, the presence of Russian-made—and manned— artillery likely caused considerable consternation for the communist bosses as well, since both sides in the diplomatic war thought it 'prudent' to avoid mentioning that the Russians and Chinese were deeply involved. Obviously, it would be difficult to maintain the illusion that the US shouldn't *"widen the war,"* if it was known that Russia and China had widened it from the outset.

AUTHOR'S OBSERVATIONS

Bullets, Beans and Body Bags

The decision, at whatever level it was made, to halt helicopter resupply and medevac flights for the 2nd Battalion, 9th Marines in Laos was tantamount—in the minds of some who participated in Operation Dewey Canyon—to abandoning the troops.

The 2nd Battalion spent a week on its feet, moving through enemy territory, tearing up facilities and wiping out communist units, without resupply, without evacuation of the wounded, and without sending the dead back home for proper burial. The Marines fought to the point of exhaustion and starvation, ultimately saving themselves by attacking a fortified supply depot and turning it into a one-stop shopping center. The rice and dried fish powder they appropriated for their own needs provided the carbs and protein they needed to continue the mission. But the absence of resupply begs the question, why?

Consider that Marine and Army helicopter crews routinely flew across the Laotian border in support of SOG units operating along the Ho Chi Minh Trail. Why then, would it not be legal to resupply an entire Marine battalion that was operating there?

Well, hold on, because this one may really surprise you. The Rules of Engagement said that local ground commanders could commit troops to eliminate communist forces that were firing on or otherwise endangering our troops. But by some interpretations, if they stayed beyond the time it took to eliminate the immediate threat, then it could be seen as *occupying* that portion of Laos and that was a big political no-no. So, an entire battalion of Marines spent an entire week on the offensive, and not once in that entire time did one single helicopter bring them water, C-Rations, ammo, body bags, or take out the wounded.

There were some comments during the research for **Victory Betrayed** that perhaps the weather was the culprit. Not so, say the Marines who were on the ground. Jay Standish and James Johnson both remember that the weather over the trail was pretty good that week, and Standish has the photos to prove it.

I guess we have to chalk it up to yet another example of the sheer idiocy of the restrictions that politicians and bureaucrats put on the people who actually do the fighting.

HOME FROM THE HILL

"As we moved the troops and guns out of Cunningham,
the lines were drawing in closer and closer."

By the beginning of March, all the battalions of the 9th Marines had obtained their major objectives. Organized enemy resistance had virtually collapsed. Most enemy troops not killed or captured had withdrawn westward, deeper into Laotian sanctuaries. There was scattered activity from small groups of the enemy throughout the operational area, but it was apparent that no further significant contacts would occur. The 9th Marines had successfully interdicted Route 922 and had captured or destroyed thousands of tons of enemy food, medical supplies, and ammunition. The equivalent of two medium artillery batteries (twelve 122mm field guns) and one light battery (four 85mm guns) had been seized, along with prime movers and munition carriers. Enemy underground headquarters, storage facilities, hospitals, and troop billeting areas, as well as fortified positions, had been overrun and a significant portion of his anti-aircraft potential was located and destroyed. In short, by 1 March, with the exception of mopping up, the 9th Marine regiment had accomplished its mission.

The final phase of Operation Dewey Canyon involved returning the regiment to Vandegrift Combat Base where it would reorganize and prepare for the next battle. The original concept of operations envisioned a leapfrogging retraction from the area of operations, with each element always under a protective artillery fan—the reverse of the technique used to get the regiment into the area of operations. This movement would have required about 10 battery displacements and, since a reasonable level of artillery ammunition had to be maintained during the leapfrog maneuver, it would have entailed approximately 25 heavy lifts per howitzer battery and five heavy lifts for the mortar battery, not including normal resupply lifts. If good weather prevailed, and helicopters were abundant, the leapfrog retraction would be accomplished in seven days.[114] The operative word in this plan was *"If."* As the operation drew to a close, several factors dictated a reappraisal of the original retraction plan. First, the weather showed no signs of improving. Second, continuation of the operation throughout the retraction phase would require an initial 100 lifts of artillery ammunition to bring stocks up to appropriate levels. That this level of lift support would not be forthcoming was evident from the daily shortfall of normal ammunition resupply during the last week of February and the first few days of March. For example, the 2nd Battalion, 12th Marines required 93 lifts on 1 March to sustain normal artillery operations of which it received 35. The battalion required 94 the following day and only two were received. Part of the discrepancy was due to marginal weather. However, a larger part was due to limited helicopter assets. In addition, the 9th Marines were scheduled to relieve the 3rd Marines in the Vandegrift-Rockpile-Route 9-Cam Lo area so that the latter could join Operation Maine Crag, which had already begun. Originally the plan envisioned the 2nd Battalion being lifted to Vandegrift on 3 March, followed by the 1st Battalion on 4 March. After the 1st Battalion was out, Battery F and the 1st Provisional Battery—which had been covering the 1st Battalion's sector of the area of operations from FSB Erskine—would move to Vandegrift, and Company G, 2nd Battalion, would close Erskine. On 5 March, the 3rd Battalion and Battery E would move to Vandegrift, leaving one company at FSB Turnage as security for an ARVN 105mm battery remaining there. On 6 March, the 2nd

VICTORY BETRAYED — Ronald Winter

ARVN Regiment would retract from its area of operations under cover of its battery on Turnage, and FSB Cunningham would be evacuated with all units going to Vandegrift. Finally, on 7 March, the ARVN battery and the one company from the 3rd Battalion would be extracted from Turnage under the cover of fixed-wing aircraft, and the retraction of the regiment would be complete.[115]

The first step in the retraction plan—the retrograde of the 2nd Battalion—went as scheduled. Everything thereafter changed. The weather turned from marginal to bad. In addition, before clearing the area of operations, III MAF tasked the 9th Marines with extracting SOG forces which had been operating in Laos. A third development was the discovery of additional cache sites in the eastern portion of the operational area which had to be searched. On 8 March, the 1st Battalion, with its huge cache exploited, began to move overland to Tam Boi. In addition, FSB Erskine was evacuated, with Battery F going to Ca Lu and the 1st Provisional Battery going to Vandegrift. Two plans were then developed, designated A and B. Ultimately, the 9th Marines implemented a modified version of Plan A, which essentially followed the same scheme as the original, but which was changed frequently as weather and other factors dictated.[116]

The weather finally broke sufficiently on 15 March to move Mortar Battery to Tam Boi, and to extract all the artillery and most of the 3rd Battalion from FSB Cunningham. On that day as well, Warren Wiedhahn was named acting Commanding Officer of the 3rd Battalion in Lt. Col. Laine's absence, and immediately took responsibility for the retrograde. Control centers established helicopter approach and retirement lanes, which permitted all batteries to fire a continuous smoke and mortar suppression program until the last gun lifted out. During the movement of the 3rd Battalion to Cunningham, Company M came under intense automatic weapons fire. During the firefight,

Private First Class Alfred M. Wilson was killed protecting a fellow Marine from a grenade. For his heroic action, Private Wilson was posthumously awarded the Medal of Honor. During their movement, batteries on Cunningham fired over 1,000 rounds, including 547 rounds on active missions and 389 rounds of smoke. But the enemy, knowing the Marines were leaving the A Shau, moved ground forces into range, placing Cunningham under a heavy mortar, small arms and RPG barrage through the withdrawal. Marco Polo Smigliani, who as noted previously had been wounded twice, was hit again, twice from RPG fragments, as his team raced for the evacuation helicopter. This time his wounds were serious enough to warrant evacuation back to the States and he spent the next six months recuperating at the Naval Hospital in Charleston, SC. In addition, the Army CH-47 Chinook helicopter carrying Warren Wiedhahn was struck in one engine by ground fire and unable to gain altitude with a full load was forced to land back inside the perimeter. *"As we moved the troops and guns out of Cunningham, the lines were drawing in closer and closer,"* Wiedhahn recalled. *"The NVA were shooting up at the helicopters from underneath when we passed over them."* Ultimately, another helicopter was able to extract the crew and passengers.

Wiedhahn was awarded the Silver Star for his heroic efforts throughout the campaign, especially in taking and holding Tam Boi, as well as his efforts to successfully carry out the retrograde of FSB Cunningham under enemy fire. Cunningham was formally shut down with the extraction of a small rear echelon unit that was brought out two days later.

> **WILSON, ALFRED M.**
>
> **Rank and organization: Private First Class, U.S. Marine Corps, Company M, 3d Battalion, 9th Marines, 3d Marine Division. Place and Date: Quang Tri Province, Republic of**

Vietnam, 3 March 1969. Entered service at: Abilene, Tex. Born: 13 January 1948, Olney, Ill.

Citation:

For conspicuous gallantry and intrepidity at the risk of his life above and beyond the call of duty while serving as a rifleman with Company M in action against hostile forces. While returning from a reconnaissance-in-force mission in the vicinity of Fire Support Base Cunningham, the 1st Platoon of Company M came under intense automatic weapons fire and a grenade attack from a well concealed enemy force. As the center of the column was pinned down, the leading squad moved to outflank the enemy. Pfc. Wilson, acting as squad leader of the rear squad, skillfully maneuvered his men to form a base of fire and act as a blocking force. In the ensuing fire fight, both his machine gunner and assistant machine gunner were seriously wounded and unable to operate their weapons. Realizing the urgent need to bring the weapon into operation again, Pfc. Wilson, followed by another marine and with complete disregard for his safety, fearlessly dashed across the fire-swept terrain to recover the weapon. As they reached the machinegun, an enemy soldier stepped from behind a tree and threw a grenade toward the 2 Marines. Observing the grenade fall between himself and the other Marine, Pfc. Wilson, fully realizing the inevitable result of his actions, shouted to his companion and unhesitating threw himself on the grenade, absorbing the full force of the explosion with his own body. His heroic actions inspired his platoon members to maximum effort as they aggressively attacked and defeated the enemy. Pfc. Wilson's indomitable courage, inspiring valor and selfless devotion to duty upheld the highest traditions of the Marine Corps and the U.S. Naval Service. He gallantly gave his life for his country.[117]

Army CH-47 "Chinook" Helicopters lifted the 3rd Provisional Battery from Cunningham to Dong Ha, the first time that heavy-lift Army CH-54 "Skycranes" had not been used to move the 155mm Marine howitzers. Following the departure of the 3rd Provisional Battery, Battery D moved to Vandegrift, as did the 3rd Battalion. With all batteries except two out of the area of operations, the 2nd Battalion, 12th Marines decentralized tactical control of Battery E on Turnage and Mortar Battery on Tam Boi, and moved to Vandegrift. To provide fire support for the 1st Battalion and Company I, 3rd Battalion, Battery E was given the mission of direct support of those units, and tactical fire direction of Mortar Battery. The 1st Battalion FSCC was given responsibility for all fire support coordination within the operational area.[118]

Marginal weather dominated the execution of the withdrawal plan to the finish. Company K and the 2nd Battalion, 12th Marines' rear echelon on Cunningham were extracted on 18 March, and the fire support base closed. By this time, the 1st Battalion had joined with SOG forces and was also ready to be extracted, but the weather closed in again, effectively isolating the battalion and exposing it to enemy ground probes and constant mortar fire. To follow the planned sequence of movements would leave the remaining units dependent on highly unpredictable weather conditions. Therefore, when the weather around Tam Boi broke on the morning of 18 March, 1st Battalion commander, Lieutenant Colonel George W. Smith, decided to extract whatever could be lifted out, weather permitting. As a result, Mortar Battery was extracted first, and thus it did not provide

VICTORY BETRAYED — Ronald Winter

covering fires for the evacuation of FSB Turnage as planned. Instead Battery E, in conjunction with fixed-wing and helicopter gunship strikes, covered the withdrawal of the 1st Battalion under heavy enemy mortar and anti-aircraft fire, and was in turn covered by fixed-wing aircraft. Harvey Barnum remembered that Battery E fired continuously for two days to cover the 1st Battalion's withdrawal and secure its own position. The retrograde of Battery E with Barnum in command, provided more examples of the often audacious but ingenious thinking that marked the entire operation. With the enemy aware that most of the Marines had returned to Vandegrift and its environs, a company-sized assault was launched at FSB Turnage. Barnum recalled that he was ordered to spike the battery's howitzers and return to Vandegrift with the remaining forces. Barnum chose to take a different approach. He was able to find several CH-53 and CH-47 helicopters to lift the battery's howitzers back to Vandegrift instead of destroying them in place. He managed to get the battery back to Vandegrift intact, much to the surprise, he said, of the division and battalion commanders. Barnum recalled that when he also arrived at Vandegrift, *"I got a phone call,"* meaning he was being called on the carpet. *"I got a few ass chewings on Dewey Canyon,"* Barnum recalled. But that came after FSB Turnage was completely cleaned of equipment, even a last bag of mail that was lying on the ground and recovered by Barnum before the last helicopter left the base. In addition to the intelligence that might have been available if the NVA had captured the mail, Barnum also remembers that *"there were letters in that bag from young Marines to their families. I couldn't just leave it there."* The NVA assault on the base continued as the last two helicopters filled with Marines left, and Barnum described a shoot-out to the very end. *"The helicopter gunners were shooting their .50 calibers and we were shooting M-79s (grenade launchers) off the rear ramp as we took off,"* he said. Operation Dewey Canyon terminated at 20:00 hours, as the last helicopter touched down at Vandegrift Combat Base.

AUTHOR'S OBSERVATIONS

Retrograde?

When viewed from the vantage point of history, it would appear that getting out of Operation Dewey Canyon was more difficult than getting into it. In any other war, there would have been more than sufficient troops involved to take the real estate, occupy the real estate and keep the real estate.

Not so in Vietnam. Which is why it sounds so ridiculous when revisionist historians say that Dewey Canyon was unsuccessful because the 9th Marines didn't permanently close down the Ho Chi Minh Trail. That wasn't the mission and if it had been the mission, it is likely the entire 3rd Marine Division would have been engaged, and probably a division of US Army troops as well.

So, once they had exploited all the hidden facilities and weapons cache sites they could find, the 9th Marines were moved back to Vandegrift Combat Base to relieve the 3rd Marines who moved on to another operation, Maine Crag, which was engaged in blocking communist units from crossing the DMZ into South Vietnam.

Just because the NVA took a beating in Dewey Canyon didn't mean all the troops were dead or incapacitated. So, the NVA made what was termed the *"retrograde"* from Dewey Canyon as difficult as possible. Until the very last day, as the last artillery pieces from E Battery were lifted out, and the remaining troops right after them, the NVA took to dropping thousands of mortar rounds and rockets into the fire bases as they were being closed down.

In the overall, it didn't matter and didn't change anything. But the NVA certainly had its pride, and like street fighters who get knocked down, but will keep coming back until they are knocked out, the NVA couldn't let it go without an "OH Yeah!" at the departing Marines. Having never been in that position I'm not sure how hard it is to yell swear words in Vietnamese when your jaw is broken and your teeth are knocked out.

BY THE NUMBERS

"The infantry and artillery are the tip of the spear.
But the communications, helicopters and logistics personnel are the shaft.
And without a strong shaft, the tip can't function."

During Dewey Canyon, supporting arms played a decisive role in the success of the operation, even accounting for the bad weather. As Harvey Barnum saw the operation, *"It was a logistics nightmare."* Nonetheless, he said, the logistics personnel back at Vandegrift who figured out myriad ways of packaging the supplies each unit needed, and the air crews who braved enemy fire and impossible flying conditions to bring in supplies and take the wounded out, *"were the heroes. For us to go that far, that rapidly, with continual movement,"* and still be supplied, was *"an eye opener,"* he said. When engaged in battle, Barnum added, *"The infantry and artillery are the tip of the spear. But the communications, helicopters and logistics personnel are the shaft. And without a strong shaft, the tip can't function."*

Throughout the operation Marine fixed-wing aircraft flew a total of 461 close air support missions, expending over 2,000 tons of ordnance. At the same time, Provisional Marine Aircraft Group 39 in Quang Tri, and Marine Aircraft Group 36 in Phu Bai, flew nearly 1,200 helicopter sorties, transporting a total of 9,121 troops and 1,533,597 pounds of cargo. On the ground, Lieutenant Colonel Scoppa's artillery fired approximately 134,000 rounds in support of Marine and South Vietnamese infantrymen. The Marines lost 130 killed and 920 wounds reported, while reporting enemy casualties of 1,617 killed, as confirmed by intact body count, and five captured. Enemy equipment losses were significant: 1,223 individual weapons, 16 artillery pieces, 73 anti-aircraft guns, 26 mortars, 104 machine guns, 92 trucks, over 807,000 rounds of ammunition, and more than 220,000 pounds of rice.

The final score, however, reached far beyond mere statistical results. The Marine strike into the Song Da Krong and A Shau valleys disrupted the organizational apparatus of Base Area 611, effectively blocking the enemy's ability to strike out at civilian and military targets to the east. Attempts to rebuild this base and reorder disrupted supply lines would be long and arduous. In reporting to General Abrams on Dewey Canyon, General Stilwell stated:

"In my possibly parochial estimate, this ranks with the most significant undertakings of the Vietnam conflict in the concept and results: striking the enemy unexpectedly in time and place, destroying an NVA base area and LOC center and pre-empting a planned NVA spring offensive somewhere in ICTZ (I Corps Tactical Zone) .... The enemy took a calculated risk in massing installations right at the border, misjudging our reach. He lost .... Above all, though, a Marine Regiment of extraordinary cohesion, skill in mountain warfare, and plain heart made Dewey Canyon a resounding success. As an independent regimental operation, projected 50KM airline from (the) nearest base and sustained in heavy combat seven weeks, it may be unparalleled. Without question, the 9th Marines' performance represents the very essence of professionals."[19] Gen. Stilwell later submitted the 9th Marines and supporting units for the Army Presidential Unit Citation.

AUTHOR'S OBSERVATIONS

That's a Ton of Stuff

So, what does a battalion of Marines do with hundreds of tons of munitions, equipment, crew-served weapons, food, medical supplies, medicines and the myriad other types of war materiel that were taken away from the North Vietnamese Army?

You call in the engineers, that's what.

What do the engineers do? They make a huge pile of stuff, some of which, being artillery rounds, makes a really, really big BOOM!, when ignited. Then they affix explosives all throughout the pile.

Then they tell everyone to "Get back, way back. No, that is NOT far enough, I said way, way, WAY back."

When everyone has complied, the engineers join them in the way, way, way back and then, KA-BOOM! Several of the Marines I interviewed for **Victory Betrayed** clearly remember the engineers destroying huge caches of enemy supplies.

And when they said they got way, way back, they meant something like a half-mile or so. And when the KA-BOOM came, they remember dirt, rocks and even shrapnel from destroyed enemy equipment raining down around them.

And they cheered. Why? You don't think Marines become Marines just for the uniforms and pretty girls do you? Marines are genetically programmed to enjoy making stuff go BOOM! That's who we are. If we are going to fight a really nasty enemy day after day, the least we should get for a reward after they are beaten is to see their stuff go BOOM!

LAOS: REPERCUSSIONS

"Marines took up positions in Laos to protect their flank
during a sweep of the area near the border."

Knowledge of the Laos incursion, ordered kept under wraps by General Abrams, found its way into the press during the first week of March, causing concern in Saigon as noted in the following memo from MACV: *We have received word from III MAF that a number of correspondents have considerable knowledge of that part of Dewey Canyon that has extended into Laos. Newsmen apparently picked up bits and pieces from troopers while sitting around talking and eating. Media involved are AP, UP, NY Times, Newsweek, AFP, and the New Yorker. We have a rumor that some of the media have photos that they claim were taken in Laos. However, we cannot confirm that any newsman or photographer actually entered Laos in the Dewey Canyon area.*[120]

Although the Laos intrusion was completely legal and conducted in accordance with the Rules of Engagement, the official line was to say nothing on the subject, diverting press attention instead to the large amounts of enemy supplies captured. On 8 March, however, Drummond Ayres, Jr., of the New York Times informed MACV that he was filing a story on Marine operations in Laos. Attempts were made to persuade Ayres to ignore the story, but it appeared in the Sunday edition of the Times the following day. While claiming that Marines had *"technically violated Laotian neutrality"* guaranteed at Geneva in 1954, and again in 1962, and ignoring the North Vietnamese position that the area was actually part of their country, not Laos, the article continued that the operations were carried out *"to protect the flanks of Marine elements maneuvering nearby along*

South Vietnam's northwestern border." Concluding, Ayres reported that *"Operation Dewey Canyon seems to indicate that allied commanders operating along borders may dip across lines to secure their flanks."* [121]

The subject was brought up again during the final news conference of Defense Secretary Melvin R. Laird's fact-finding mission to Vietnam. Asked if American troops had been operating in Laos during the last week, Laird said: *"I would not confirm that they were there now, but I would certainly say that there have been operations in which it has been necessary in order to protect American fighting forces—that border being a very indefinite border—it may have been transgressed by American forces in carrying out this responsibility."* [122]

The Secretary noted that the decision to permit operations inside Laos had been reviewed at the highest level and approved by General Abrams on the basis of the *"safety of our men."* He further explained that *"Marines took up positions in Laos to protect their flank during a sweep of the area near the border."* Secretary Laird's statements acknowledging the American incursion into Laos caused *"embarrassment"* in Vientiane. The Laotian Government immediately sought to counter the Secretary's remarks by issuing a communique *"clearly designed to confine the controversy to a discussion of a single incident rather than to the general implications for Laotian neutrality."* The controversy did not end there. In 1970 and again in 1973, the Marine incursion into Laos during Operation Dewey Canyon came to the fore, both times in connection with Congressional hearings on Vietnam. [123]

CONCLUSION

The heroes of Dewey Canyon are fast fading away. Many have long since passed. But for nearly 60 days in what has been accurately described as a Green Hell, they proved themselves far superior to an enemy that some in the media portrayed as invincible. Battles usually are fluid events, not static, and the heart of the combatants, as well as the ingenuity and courage of the commanders has much to do with the outcome. Directed by a General and led by a Colonel who themselves defined audacity and integrity, as well as independence of thought and action, they went places that supposedly were inaccessible, they fought against odds that supposedly were unbeatable. And they prevailed.

Major Gen. Raymond Davis and Col. Robert Barrow were highly intelligent men—in a time when the media beat a considerably different drum regarding the wisdom of serving in the military. They had the presence of mind to actually read the Rules of Engagement and apply them to the conditions in the field. Hence the successful, and legal, incursion into Laos by the 2nd Battalion. They took the fight from the enemy's front yard right into his sanctuary, a supposedly inviolate area where the North Vietnamese could move and stage troops and supplies with relative impunity, and a retreat where they could recover from the constant beatings put upon them by US and other allied forces. Yet it was that same incursion as part of operation Dewey Canyon that provided the best example

VICTORY BETRAYED — Ronald Winter

of the unconscionable meddling in military operations in Vietnam by politicians, diplomats and bureaucrats. As many of the survivors of Dewey Canyon, including Jay Standish, are quick to point out, *"They never had to spend one instant of their lives living with the consequences of their interference."* Of particular note was the reaction of the US Ambassador to Laos, William H. Sullivan, when the media reported that the Marines had *"violated"* Laotian neutrality.

Seven years after the neutrality agreement was signed, the North Vietnamese, with help from Russia and China, had transformed eastern Laos, and Cambodia too, into an essential part of their military supply network, in a blatant and continuing violation of Article 4 of the agreement. And by occupying that portion of Laos west of Khe Sanh and the A Shau valley, even flying the North Vietnamese flag there, the communist north considered any pre-existing border invalid, further negating the concept of Laotian neutrality in that area. Yet, when word circulated that the Marines had crossed an invisible—and possibly non-existent—line in a remote and nearly inaccessible jungle to destroy the enemy's ability to kill American troops in South Vietnam, the fear of media reaction in American political circles was so pervasive that Ambassador Sullivan subsequently apologized to the Laotian Premier and assured him that the United States would avoid any further hostilities in Laotian territory. Five decades later Sullivan's apology still irritates many of the Marines, who fought in Operation Dewey Canyon.

"We won the war on the ground, just so the politicians could lose it back in Washington," groused former Lance Corporal Marco Polo Smigliani. His point of view was echoed by former Lieutenant Miles Davis, son of Major General Raymond Davis. *"We adhered to an invisible line in an impenetrable jungle, while the other side completely ignored it, just so diplomats and politicians could keep their chins up on the international stage,"* he said.

VICTORY BETRAYED — Ronald Winter

Harvey Barnum, who spent years lecturing on the lessons learned from Dewey Canyon, alongside Gen. Davis and Col. Barrow, said that *"when the determination is made to commit forces, the officers on the ground should be allowed to use all the weapons they have at their disposal. All their might, and all their weapons. Too many politicians think they can run wars from Washington,"* he said. *"But Vietnam was not lost by the military. We won all the major battles. It was lost in D. C. Don't give the order to land the landing force, don't commit troops, if you don't have the will to win."*

Yet, for all the political meddling, the Marines of Dewey Canyon to this day are proud of their accomplishments and those of their brother Marines. Smigliani spent six months in the Naval Hospital in Charleston, S.C., and after release returned to his home village in Italy, where he received a hero's welcome. *"The whole village turned out. It must have been 800 people. The area television station even came to interview me. It was so different from what most of my friends from the 9th Marines encountered when they came home."* Smigliani left the Marines, and in April of 1975 was serving in the Merchant Marines off the coast of Saigon as South Vietnam collapsed, and terrified refugees began the saga of what became the *"boat people."* Yet, in retrospect, Smigliani's best memory of his time in the Marines involved Operation Dewey Canyon, he said years later. *"I remember meeting some of the most wonderful men. Not heroes, just incredible people,"* in the 9th Marines. *"They were totally dedicated to each other."*

Navy Cross recipient James Johnson has similar feelings about his time in Dewey Canyon. But there was more to Johnson's loyalty to the cause—his belief in what it means to be a Marine, and how that impacts an individual's actions during combat. Johnson left active duty after he returned from a 4th tour in Vietnam, but a decade later he returned to the Marines, with direct intervention from Col. Barrow, who by then was Gen. Barrow and Commandant of the

240

VICTORY BETRAYED — Ronald Winter

Marine Corps. Johnson became a drill instructor at the Marine Corps Recruit Depot in San Diego, and every night when he had the overnight duty he would drill one simple but effective lesson into the recruits' minds. Johnson would pace from one end of the squad bay to the other, reminding his charges that their jobs would be *"to find the enemy, close with the enemy, and kill the enemy."* He would end every training day with the same lesson, *"Close and kill. Close and kill. Close and kill."* Lights out.

Johnson considers the 9th Marines he served with to be the epitome of the fighting Marine, and he had the utmost respect for Gen. Davis and Col. Barrow. *"If you wanted to be a Marine, that's what the 9th was all about,"* Johnson said. *"But it didn't happen by accident. General Davis took lumps of clay, put all the right people in the right places,"* and the force fighting in Dewey Canyon was the result. *"The people involved in Dewey Canyon were Marines' Marines."*

Ultimately, despite the complications forced on those who fought in the Da Krong and A Shau valleys—and Laos—by the political establishment, they still accomplished their goals, exceeded all expectations, forced the NVA out of their own sanctuaries, and dispelled any notions of dry season attacks in I Corps by communist forces in 1969. Put bluntly by Col. Wesley Fox, more than four decades after he was awarded the Medal of Honor, *"The enemy was not ready for us. They never considered even Marines sticking their necks out in that place, at that time, under those conditions. But we caught them with their pants down. And we kicked butt."*

EPILOGUE

When Jay Standish and James Johnson crossed the border from Laos back into South Vietnam with the 2nd Battalion, 9th Marines as the Laotian incursion ended, they believed that a major victory had been won, and *"we had changed the course of the war."*

There was good reason to feel that way, considering the rout that the Marines had put on the North Vietnamese and their Chinese and Russian overseers. In Dewey Canyon the Marines lost 130 killed in action over two months, and suffered 900 wounds, with some Marines wounded as many as four times. In turn they killed more than 1,600 enemy troops, as confirmed by intact body count, and captured or destroyed thousands of tons of arms, food, and medicine, took two entire artillery batteries away from the communists—both North Vietnamese and Russians—and destroyed facilities that had been drilled into solid rock years before. The Laotian raid was entirely legal since the communists had been shooting at and killing Marines using Russian artillery from across the border. As the commanders noted, the Rules of Engagement allowed them to cross the border to engage the enemy if our troops were under attack or in danger from forces there.

The number of enemy killed is deliberately couched in the term *"intact body count,"* since US forces were not allowed to count the retreating communists killed as they ran for their Laotian sanctuaries, nor those killed by artillery and air strikes, or the dead buried in collapsed bunkers and tunnels. The American media had established its own set of rules early on in what was called a "War of Attrition" for counting enemy dead—either produce intact bodies of dead communist soldiers or they didn't count.

The sheer stupidity of that concept is staggering, considering that artillery and bombs literally evaporate not just individual bodies, but entire units that are caught in the cone of fire. In fact, the body count rules imposed by the media at that time revealed either an appalling lack of knowledge of battlefield realities, or an equally appalling level of complicity with communist goals.

Of equal importance was the fact that while the Marines were slugging it out in the A Shau and Da Krong valleys and Laos, forces were at work in the Washington D. C. conference rooms and the halls of Congress that would ultimately undo all they fought to achieve. Literally, as the first troops were ferried into the Dewey Canyon Area of Operations, Richard Nixon was taking the oath of office in Washington, and his promise to "end the war" that helped get him elected, soon would impact all of the nearly 550,000 American troops in Vietnam.

Instead of capitalizing on the successes of Dewey Canyon and other battles, the Nixon administration announced the withdrawal of US forces, giving communists a reason to keep fighting, knowing that what they couldn't achieve on the battlefield, was possible through political means.

Nixon had been somewhat vague during his campaign about the details of that promise—he called it a secret plan to win the war—but later in the spring of 1969 he showed how simplistic his idea of "Peace with Honor" would be. He announced that America would begin withdrawing troops immediately! Not everyone, and not all at once, but by summer of 1969 the 9th Marines and thousands of other American troops began the exodus from the war zone.

VICTORY BETRAYED — Ronald Winter

Why Nixon chose this drastic and ill-advised step is the subject of considerable debate among military and political historians. But one theory that is not generally discussed has to do with the Straits of Malacca. By the time Operation Dewey Canyon was complete, the straits were secure. Prime Minister Suharto had vanquished Indonesian communists, the remaining communist forces in Malaysia were reduced to harassment operations, and shipping was free to traverse the straits unimpeded.

The media gave scant attention to Suharto's overwhelming victory against the communists, but the impact Nixon's announcement had on the fighting in Vietnam was immediate. The communist military commanders, although reeling from astounding defeats all across the south, were ordered by their political bosses—sensing a significant weakening not of battlefield strength, but of political will in the US—to continue the fight. After Dewey Canyon, which capped an entire year of massive losses by the communists beginning with the Tet Offensive of 1968 and continuing unabated for the next year and more, communist generals reportedly were lobbying their political bosses to surrender, or at least to call for a truce. Their intentions were not honorable. They wanted to stop the fighting so they could reinforce and regroup, convince the free-world forces to stand down, and renew the fighting later, when South Vietnam was more vulnerable.

Nixon provided them with all they had hoped to achieve, without the communists losing face by suing for peace, and the generals were ordered to continue fighting, losses be damned. Meanwhile North Vietnam was able to continue resupplying and reinforcing its dwindling forces, because US politicians and diplomats continued to insist that American and other free world troops stay within the borders of South Vietnam.

VICTORY BETRAYED — Ronald Winter

In 1970, smarting from criticism over his troop withdrawals, and from his announcement of the vaunted "Vietnamization" program, whereby South Vietnam would take over more of the military burden, Nixon ordered US forces to invade eastern Cambodia and interdict the Ho Chi Minh Trail. Good idea, wrong place. The key chokepoint on the trail was not in Cambodia, but hundreds of miles north in Tchepone, Laos. Also, attempting to assuage political opponents in the US, Nixon announced exactly how far into Cambodia the American forces would push, and how long they would stay there. In the boxing world this is known as *"telegraphing your punches."*

The Cambodian incursion was successful as far as it went, but it also gave the communists time to remove their forces and supplies to sanctuaries deeper in Cambodia. Within months the communists were back in their border refuges, resupplied, reinforced and ready to continue fighting.

But there also were political ramifications in the US, and in late 1970 Congress passed the Cooper-Church Amendment—named for virulent anti-Vietnam War senators John Sherman Cooper (Republican, Kentucky) and Frank Church (Democrat, Idaho)—which prohibited US forces from crossing the border into Cambodia in the future. Their amendment to the 1970 Foreign Assistance Act didn't specifically say so, but the resolution also was taken to mean that US forces could not enter Laos again either. Church also sponsored an amendment to prohibit the use of US ground troops in Laos and Thailand.

In February 1971, one month after the Cooper-Church Amendment was enacted, and two years after Operation Dewey Canyon, South Vietnamese forces, minus American field support and adequate air support, attempted to take Tchepone. Attacking with a force of 12,000 infantry, armor, and artillery in an operation code-

VICTORY BETRAYED — Ronald Winter

named Lam Song 719 or Dewey Canyon II, the ARVN launched its cross-border offensive while thousands of US troops assembled on the Khe Sanh plateau. The American show of force had no teeth, however, since they couldn't move one inch into Laos.

Roughly 20 miles or so west of Khe Sanh, Tchepone, not only was a transportation hub for the trail, it was a chokepoint, and not just any chokepoint. It was THE chokepoint for the entire network. And everyone knew it. Communist generals, writing their memoirs after the war, questioned why we never took Tchepone, noting that if we had, the war would have ended in six months tops because they would have no way to resupply and reinforce their forces in the south.

But the ARVN plans were leaked to the north by spies and the communist garrison protecting Tchepone was massively reinforced. By the time the southern forces were within sight of their objective, they were counter-attacked by a North Vietnamese force of more than 60,000 and were thrown back. Most southern forces fought well and valiantly, costing the communists 20,000 troops KIA. But some broke and ran, instead of conducting a fighting withdrawal, and of course the American media was on hand in South Vietnam to film them hanging off the skids of evacuation helicopters. There was little to no filming of the units that marched back into the south.

Northern communists were emboldened by their victory in Lam Song 719, and believing the US would no longer support the southern forces, launched a massive invasion in the spring of 1972, after the majority of US combat troops had long since left. The invasion consisted of approximately 250,000 troops including armor and artillery. But this time the US did use its air power to support the south, and after the initial onslaught that pushed the southern troops back nearly 50 miles from the DMZ, counterattacking southerners turned the tide, forcing the communists back across the entire invasion front.

After several months of hard fighting the communist forces were decisively defeated. In the 1990s, researchers perusing Russian documents after the fall of the Soviet Union discovered North Vietnam lost an estimated 150,000 troops, plus half of all its armor and artillery.

The leader of the failed communist invasion was the top communist general, Vo Nguyen Giap, who beat the French in the 1950s. But Giap was defeated in the disastrous Tet Offensive against the Americans in 1968, in which the communists lost some 70,000 troops including 40,000 Viet Cong out of the 75,000 who attacked in the initial assault. He also failed in his effort to overrun Khe Sanh in the same period. He also lost thousands of troops after the communists occupied the undefended city of Hue, and butchered as many as 8,000 inhabitants, mostly civilians. Giap survived those defeats but after he failed spectacularly in the 1972 Easter Invasion, he was fired, and placed under house arrest for the next three years.

Nonetheless, instead of supporting the south in a final push to rid the country of all communist forces by eliminating a pocket of survivors holed up in the A Shau valley in late 1972, the Nixon administration refused. Once again diplomats prevailed, based on the belief that battlefield mercy would strengthen their negotiating positions, ignoring the basic fact that the best bargaining position in war is total victory.

However, the communists refused to budge, seeing Nixon's reluctance to obliterate their forces as weakness. This led to Nixon's ordering the Christmas bombings of 1972. American B-52 bombers conducted around-the-clock bombing of the Hanoi-Haiphong area for 11 days, after which the communists agreed to return to the bargaining table. Giap later wrote in his memoirs that if the US bombing had persisted for two more days, the northern communists would have surrendered.

The result was the Paris Peace Accords of March 1973, which were vehemently opposed by the South Vietnamese, because, among many other reasons, it gave full status to the Viet Cong, who had ceased to exist as a viable fighting force after massive losses in the 1968 Tet Offensive and the ill-fated follow-up Mini-Tet in May. The South Vietnamese also objected to the full withdrawal of all US fighting units and signed primarily on Nixon's promise for full military support should the communists attack again. Nixon also promised to continue resupply of parts, equipment and ammunition from the US.

Like the Agreement on Laotian Neutrality, the Paris Peace Accords were rendered moot within three months of their implementation in March 1973. But this time it was the US Congress that betrayed its armed forces and allies by passing in June of that year the Case-Church Resolution, named for Senators Clifford P. Case (R-NJ) and Frank Church (D-ID). That amendment eliminated all military support for South Vietnam. It took Congress only 90 days to betray an ally that had shown its willingness and ability to stay free and independent if we stood by our promise to provide effective support.

The following year Congress passed the Foreign Assistance Act of 1974 which contained provisions to eliminate all aid to South Vietnam, and the die was cast. On April 10, 1975, President Gerald Ford asked a joint session of Congress to allocate funds for the defense of South Vietnam. Many in Congress turned their backs on the president and walked out on him. By April 30, 1975 South Vietnam, abandoned and out of bullets, was overrun, as the US Congress stood fast in its refusal to provide any aid.

VICTORY BETRAYED — Ronald Winter

Following the fall of Saigon, communist forces also defeated free world governments in Laos and Cambodia and the slaughter was on. Despite the incredible claim in a recent Ken Burns documentary on Vietnam that, *"the expected bloodbath did not materialize,"* the facts are different. A million South Vietnamese were imprisoned in concentration camps, referred to by the media and other communist supporters in the US government as re-education camps, and at least 161,000 were executed, tortured, blown up or worked to death.

Two million south Vietnamese fled on the South China Sea and Gulf of Thailand, becoming the infamous boat people. At least 300,000 are believed to have died. Laos was taken over by the Pathet Lao communists, vicious terrorists who imposed a reign so restrictive that at least 10 percent of the country's population of 20 million was killed or fled to Thailand.

In Cambodia the true meaning of a communist takeover was quickly on display as the Khmer Rouge began wholesale slaughter and butchery that left at least two million people dead. When refugees began showing up on foreign shores, the extent of the slaughter leaked out with two results. In the US, the media and politicians pointed the finger at the military and said those who fought the Vietnam War were to blame.

On the foreign scene, pressure was put on the communists to ease up. They didn't. So, in 1979 the Vietnamese communists who are backed by Russia, invaded the Cambodian communists who are backed by the Chinese, to make them stop the slaughter, which angered the Chinese who invaded Vietnam to make them withdraw from Cambodia.

The imprisonments in Vietnam, that supposedly were to last for only 90 days to help the southerners *"readjust"* to the new realities, went on for more than a decade. Following the fall of three countries

VICTORY BETRAYED — Ronald Winter

in Southeast Asia, at least 3 million people were murdered by the communists.

The communist dictator and mass murderer, Josef Stalin, is quoted as saying *"the death of an individual is a tragedy, the death of a million is a statistic."* The carnage in Southeast Asia easily can be seen as 3 million tragedies. And the bureaucrats, diplomats and politicians who caused this horror had the temerity to blame the military. Which shouldn't surprise us. After Operation Dewey Canyon, which was an overwhelming victory, the ambassador to Laos, William Sullivan apologized to his Laotian counterpart for the Marines stepping on their territory. What incredible, unspeakable gall! A US ambassador apologizing for US Marines doing what Marines do, doing what Marines are supposed to do!

It is not enough to say the bureaucracy undermined the military, even as it won every single major battle in the war. It is not enough to point out that, although America lost 58,000 people in that war, the communists lost at least 1.5 million northern troops. Those are their figures. We also have to realize that the fall of Vietnam, Laos and Cambodia was not the end and this is not ancient history. It is incumbent upon all of us to be aware of the long-term issues that confront us. Control of free trade shipping routes is as important today as it was 50 years ago, and the recent mining of the Straits of Hormuz by Iran, as well as the capture of foreign oil tankers there, is a classic example.

Since the fall of South Vietnam and the carnage that ensued as communists overran that portion of Southeast Asia, it has been 'popular' in the media and political circles to chant, *"No More Vietnams!"* Unfortunately, what happened in Vietnam was neither the first nor the last time that politicians and diplomats intervened in America's wars. It was politics that stopped Gen. George Patton in

VICTORY BETRAYED — Ronald Winter

Germany, as the government ceded huge swaths of Eastern Europe to the Russian Communists. Two generations of non-Russians lived and died under the dictators' boots due to that decision.

It was the US government that made it illegal for US forces to bomb Chinese staging areas and anti-aircraft artillery sites on the Chinese side of the Yalu River during the Korean War. This enabled the Chinese to continually reinforce and resupply their armies in Korea, leading to the armistice in 1953 and a communist North Korean regime that exists to this day.

After Vietnam, and after the terrorist attacks of Sept. 11, 2001, America fought wars against Islamic-terrorists in Afghanistan and Iraq, scoring decisive victories on both battlefields. Yet in both cases the military victories were obscured by political meddling that led to the withdrawal of American forces in Iraq in 2011, and the rise of the brutal Islamic-terrorist group known as ISIS.

In Afghanistan the Taliban that was crushed in a matter of months in 2002, re-emerged with support from Pakistan, very similar to that given to the Vietnamese communists. More than 19 years after the US military first entered Afghanistan, and more than a decade after the American forces left, leaving Afghan security to NATO, we are back and have been for years. Yet, Americans still are dying there, even as mindless Rules of Engagement hamstring our troops, and diplomatic maneuvering prevents the military from taking out Taliban sanctuaries in Pakistan.

There are ways to undo this, of course. If, as reported, only 15 percent of today's forces see direct battlefield action, then pare down the military to those who are fighting or directly supporting them. Ensure we have enough aircraft, ships, submarines, tanks, artillery, cyber and satellite security, drones and related equipment to fight wars, not fight the bureaucracy.

VICTORY BETRAYED — Ronald Winter

Rewrite the Rules of Engagement to reflect those dictated by the Geneva Convention of 1949, the Hague Convention and their predecessors. They were more than enough to dictate proper battlefield behavior and care for civilians caught in war zones. The US fought two World Wars without the necessity of Judge Advocate General (JAG) lawyers looking over the shoulders of our fighting forces, and putting many in jail for minor violations of unnecessary Rules of Engagement. Get these people off of the backs of our military.

Finally, adhere to the US Constitution. If war is necessary let it be debated in Congress and approved by a majority of both houses. Let the President, as Commander-in-Chief give marching orders to his generals and admirals, which should include a definition of victory. Don't meddle with command unless the commanders are not succeeding. And keep the media out of the war zone unless they are military combat correspondents.

If we really want *"No More Vietnams,"* then stop the politicians, bureaucrats and diplomats from wielding the same power they did in Vietnam, and for which they have no Congressional authorization. Give them something else to do while the warriors fight the battles, and keep the non-combatants off the battlefield and out of the chain of command.

Simply put, get everyone who is not fighting the war the hell out of the way. And stay the hell out of the way until the war is won.

AUTHOR'S OBSERVATIONS

A Post-Dewey Canyon Timeline

Jan. 22, 1969 9th Marines Launch Operation Dewey Canyon.

March 22, 1969 Dewey Canyon ends.

Dec. 1970 Congress passes Cooper-Church Amendment outlawing US military operations outside the borders of South Vietnam.

Feb. 1971 South Vietnamese Army launches Lam Song 719, in an attempt to take Tchepone in Laos and permanently block Ho Chi Minh Trail. Operation fails after nearly 6 weeks due to lack of ground and air support from the US, and massive counter-attack by 60,000 communist troops.

Easter 1972 North Vietnam invades South Vietnam using 250,000 troops. Initially successful, the combination of South Vietnamese ground forces including tanks and artillery, supported by US air power, eventually repel the invasion. Cost to the north is estimated at 150,000 troops KIA and half of all armor and artillery destroyed. Communist Gen. Vo Nguyen Giap is fired and arrested.

December 1972 US Launches around-the-clock bombing of Hanoi and Haiphong by B-52 bombers to force communists to bargaining table. Bombing is halted after 11 days when the North Vietnamese agree to resume talks. Communist leaders reveal after the war that they would have surrendered unconditionally if bombing had continued for two more days.

January 1973 Paris Peace agreement is reached.

March 1973 Paris Peace Accords go into effect.

June 1973 US Congress passes Case-Church Amendment, negating Paris Accords.

August 1974 President Nixon resigns, President Ford takes office.

Nov. 1974 - Congress passes Foreign Assistance Act of 1974, abandoning South Vietnam.

January 1975 North Vietnam begins limited invasion of South Vietnam.

April 10, 1975 President Ford asks Congress to fund military action to support South Vietnam. Many in Congress turn backs on Ford and walk out.

April 30, 1975 South Vietnam, alone and abandoned, falls to the communists. In the next decade an estimated 3,000,000 Southeast Asians died at the hands of the communists.

AUTHOR'S OBSERVATIONS

Medals of Honor

A total of four Medals of Honor (not *Congressional* Medal of Honor, there is no such medal) were awarded to members of the 9th Marines during Operation Dewey Canyon. Three were for actions in South Vietnam, while one, for Cpl. William D. Morgan was for heroism on the Ho Chi Minh Trail. But even the nation's highest award for bravery and heroism under fire was not immune from the bureaucratic and political maneuvering that marked virtually every aspect of the fighting in the Vietnam War.

Although the action that cost Cpl. Morgan his life clearly took place with the 2nd Battalion, 9th Marines during the Laotian incursion, and far more than just a few steps from the border with Vietnam, so there is no question of mistaken location, the citation claims the fighting took place in Quang Tri Province.

It isn't as if the North Vietnamese didn't know the Marines had crossed the line into Laos, were killing communists and breaking their stuff. The entire North Vietnamese Army was frantically attempting to find out how far the 9th would go and how long they would stay. It can safely be presumed that the Laotian incursion caused its share of stomach ulcers in the communist hierarchy.

But it wasn't the communists who had an issue with the Marines doing what Marines do. It was the politicians and bureaucrats back home, who were more concerned about how it would appear in the media than whether the raid would be successful.

Doctoring the citation for Cpl. Morgan's Medal of Honor, as much as anything else in the Vietnam War, shows the unconscionable interference that loomed over the military's attempts to put the war to an end once and for all.

AUTHOR'S OBSERVATIONS

The First Amendment

There are many aspects of the Vietnam War that can be described as reprehensible, the vast majority of which have to do with political and bureaucratic interference.

But as bad as they were, the media and its interminable opposition to the military, the war, and anyone who supported either, arguably is the worst offender and the most reprehensible. Not everyone, and not every news outlet. But the big ones who made the most impact on the American public, operated in an area of self-induced hypocrisy that in many cases can be seen as outright treason.

We need look no further than the media's insistence that it print or broadcast stories about the 9th Marines crossing the line into Laos to wipe out communist positions and supplies—while the Marines were still in the field, still engaged against the enemy and still taking casualties.

Other than idiotic attempts to be 'first with the story,' there was no overriding reason to publish it prior to the Marines finishing Operation Dewey Canyon, unless it was to pass information to the communists under the guise of Freedom of the Press. This should come as no surprise, since the media was lying about, and undermining the US war effort, even before Walter Cronkite hustled over to Saigon after the Tet Offensive of 1968 and falsely averred that the war was at a stalemate.

Two decades after Dewey Canyon, American 'journalists' Peter Jennings and Chris Wallace told a PBS interviewer that if they accompanied an enemy patrol, and saw it setting up an ambush on American and allied forces, they would remain silent and let their countrymen die. Why? Because they maintain, *"I'm not an American first, I'm a reporter first."*

The New York Times ran at least two stories on Dewey Canyon, one in early March 1969, the other in 1973 when covering John Kerry's bogus Winter Soldier investigation. The first, with the dateline—Dong Ha—which was some 50 kilometers from the battle, gave away Marine positions and intents to the enemy. The second, flat out lied to its readers by falsely claiming that half of the Marines in the 2nd Battalion, 9th Marines who ventured into Laos were casualties. Some 500 Marines crossed the border into Laos with 8 KIA and about 30 wounded. Not even close to half!

Is it just me or is it reasonable to ask?

1. Why would American reporters go on a patrol with enemy forces?

AND

2. Where do they think their guarantee of a free press comes from?

If I recall correctly it is from the First Amendment of the document that lays out American governance, called the US Constitution. And accompanying enemy forces to write propaganda about their side is nothing less than treason. There is no guarantee that exercising freedom of the press means putting American lives, goals and objectives in danger.

Anyone who thinks this was just a "Nam thing," obviously hasn't watched a political press conference where the media act like a pack of snarling self-aggrandizing junk-yard dogs, with no couth, no self-esteem and no value to the majority of Americans. As if their behavior isn't bad enough, anyone who has watched an entire press conference, and then sees how the media spins it to fit their political agendas has little recourse but to conclude that what is called the Mainstream Media is not representing mainstream America, now or then.

258

ENDNOTES

[1] https://business.un.org/en/entities/13

[2] https://www.weforum.org/agenda/2014/05/world-most-important-trade-route/

[3] https://www.cia.gov/library/readingroom/docs/CIA-RDP85T00875R001100130038-1.pdf

[4] https://www.britannica.com/event/Vietnam-War

[5] Agence France-Presse 9-10-1977

[6] https://en.wikipedia.org/wiki/1970_United_States_Census

[7] https://www.history.com/news/vietnam-war-combatants#section_4

[8] https://www.washingtonpost.com/archive/politics/1989/05/17/china-admits-combat-in-vietnam-war/6b9cb8a4-4d18-48bf-80d2-bea80f64057c/

[9] The Path to War, Marines in the Vietnam War Commemorative Series

[10] The Path to War, Marines in the Vietnam War Commemorative Series

[11] https://en.wikipedia.org/wiki/Operation_Dewey_Canyon

[12] https://www.historynet.com/vietnam-war-operation-dewey-canyon.htm

[13] U. S. Marines in Vietnam High Mobility and Standdown1969 by Charles R. Smith
CHAPTER 2

[14] U. S. Marines in Vietnam High Mobility and Standdown1969 by Charles R. Smith

[15] Hill of Angels, US Marines and the Battle for Con Thien pgs. 4,5. USMC Marines in the Vietnam War

[16] https://www.revolvy.com/main/index.php?s=North%20Vietnamese%20invasion%20of%20Laos&item_type=topic

[17] Operation Dewey Canyon, Leatherneck Magazine, Page 29, April 2014

[18] U. S. Marines in Vietnam High Mobility and Standdown1969 by Charles R. Smith

[19] U. S. Marines in Vietnam High Mobility and Standdown1969 by Charles R. Smith

[20] https://www.usni.org/magazines/proceedings/1970/may/marine-corps-operations-vietnam-1968

[21] Cavalry of the Sky by Lynn Montross Copyright 1954 Harper & Brothers

[22] https://www.usni.org/magazines/proceedings/1970/may/marine-corps-operations-vietnam-1968

[23] https://www.historynet.com/vietnam-war-operation-dewey-canyon.htm

[24] https://www.usni.org/magazines/proceedings/1970/may/marine-corps-operations-vietnam-1968

[25] Interview with Miles Davis summer 2014

[26] U. S. Marines in Vietnam High Mobility and Standdown1969 by Charles R. Smith

[27] U. S. Marines in Vietnam High Mobility and Standdown1969 by Charles R. Smith

[28] U. S. Marines in Vietnam High Mobility and Standdown1969 by Charles R. Smith

[29] U. S. Marines in Vietnam High Mobility and Standdown1969 by Charles R. Smith

[30] U. S. Marines in Vietnam High Mobility and Standdown1969 by Charles R. Smith

[31] Mike Green, used with permission.

[32] https://www.usni.org/magazines/proceedings/1970/may/marine-corps-operations-vietnam-1968

[33] U. S. Marines in Vietnam High Mobility and Standdown1969 by Charles R. Smith

[34] https://www.historynet.com/vietnam-war-operation-dewey-canyon.htm

[35] U. S. Marines in Vietnam High Mobility and Standdown1969 by Charles R. Smith

[36] U. S. Marines in Vietnam High Mobility and Standdown1969 by Charles R. Smith

[37] Interview with Warren Wiedhahn 2015

[38] https://en.wikipedia.org/wiki/Operation_Dewey_Canyon#cite_note-Smith-2

[39] U. S. Marines in Vietnam High Mobility and Standdown1969 by Charles R. Smith

[40] U. S. Marines in Vietnam High Mobility and Standdown1969 by Charles R. Smith

[41] Gen Raymond G. Davis, Comments on draft ms, Aug86 [Vietnam 69 Comment File, MCHC, Washington, D.C.]

[42] U. S. Marines in Vietnam High Mobility and Standdown1969 by Charles R. Smith

[43] Interview with MGySgt. (ret.) Jack Payne, Memphis, TN, June 2014.

[44] U. S. Marines in Vietnam High Mobility and Standdown1969 by Charles R. Smith

[45] Interview with Lt. Col. (ret.) James Loop, Memphis TN, June 14, 2014

[46] Interview with Col. (ret.) Joseph Snyder, August 18, 2015.

[47] U. S. Marines in Vietnam High Mobility and Standdown1969 by Charles R. Smith

[48] Lt. John Cochenour interview and documents

[49] Material supplied by former LCpl Alan Sargent

[50] U. S. Marines in Vietnam High Mobility and Standdown1969 by Charles R. Smith

[51] U. S. Marines in Vietnam High Mobility and Standdown1969 by Charles R. Smith

[52] https://www.mca-marines.org/leatherneck/2014/04/operation-dewey-canyon

[53] Interview with Miles Davis, Sept. 16, 2014

[54] U. S. Marines in Vietnam High Mobility and Standdown1969 by Charles R. Smith

[55] Interview with John Wilkes, Jan. 7, 2020

[56] U. S. Marines in Vietnam High Mobility and Standdown1969 by Charles R. Smith

[57] U. S. Marines in Vietnam High Mobility and Standdown1969 by Charles R. Smith

[58] http://www.marinemedals.com/noonanthomas.htm

[59] U. S. Marines in Vietnam High Mobility and Standdown1969 by Charles R. Smith

[60] U. S. Marines in Vietnam High Mobility and Standdown1969 by Charles R. Smith

[61] https://www.avgeekery.com/bet-you-didnt-know-these-5-things-about-the-sea-knight/?fbclid=IwAR3gc7XdnQObTi4VL3kDddGQBumdX20gki6uHUyY5uwPNiRxs6vaiQujTAU

[62] https://animals.fandom.com/wiki/Northern_Buffed-cheeked_Gibbon

[63] U. S. Marines in Vietnam High Mobility and Standdown1969 by Charles R. Smith

[64] U. S. Marines in Vietnam High Mobility and Standdown1969 by Charles R. Smith

[65] U. S. Marines in Vietnam High Mobility and Standdown1969 by Charles R. Smith

[66]U. S. Marines in Vietnam High Mobility and Standdown1969 by Charles R. Smith

[67]Interviews with Fred Penning June 2014, October 2015.

[68]U. S. Marines in Vietnam High Mobility and Standdown1969 by Charles R. Smith

[69]U. S. Marines in Vietnam High Mobility and Standdown1969 by Charles R. Smith

[70]U. S. Marines in Vietnam High Mobility and Standdown1969 by Charles R. Smith

[71]U. S. Marines in Vietnam High Mobility and Standdown1969 by Charles R. Smith

[72]U. S. Marines in Vietnam High Mobility and Standdown1969 by Charles R. Smith

[73]https://www.mca-marines.org/leatherneck/2014/04/operation-dewey-canyon

[74]Interview with Col. (ret.) Harvey Barnum Dec. 21, 2014

[75]U. S. Marines in Vietnam High Mobility and Standdown1969 by Charles R. Smith

[76]U. S. Marines in Vietnam High Mobility and Standdown1969 by Charles R. Smith

[77]Interview with Col. Harvey Barnum

[78]SAPPER ATTACK ON FSB CUNNINGHAM by Michael Conroy

[79]Recollections from Lt. John Cochenour

[80]SAPPER ATTACK ON FSB CUNNINGHAM by Michael Conroy

[81]https://catalog.archives.gov/OpaAPI/media/2432068/content/arcmedia/usmc/035/00000221.pdf Pg. 8

[82]James L. Johnson Navy Cross Citation

[83]Series of interviews with James Johnson in 2105 and 2016

[84]http://www.marinemedals.com/foxwesley.htm

[85]Interview with Col. (ret.) Warren Wiedhahn 14 August, 2015

[86]Interview with George Allen, Jan 10, 2020.

[87]U. S. Marines in Vietnam High Mobility and Standdown1969 by Charles R. Smith

[88]U. S. Marines in Vietnam High Mobility and Standdown1969 by Charles R. Smith

[89]U. S. Marines in Vietnam High Mobility and Standdown1969 by Charles R. Smith

[90]U. S. Marines in Vietnam High Mobility and Standdown1969 by Charles R. Smith

[91]U. S. Marines in Vietnam High Mobility and Standdown1969 by Charles R. Smith

[92]U. S. Marines in Vietnam High Mobility and Standdown1969 by Charles R. Smith

[93]U. S. Marines in Vietnam High Mobility and Standdown1969 by Charles R. Smith

[94]U. S. Marines in Vietnam High Mobility and Standdown1969 by Charles R. Smith

[95]Geer, Jeff (30 March 2005). "Neutrality not the answer". www.taipeitimes.com. Taipei Times.

[96]U. S. Marines in Vietnam High Mobility and Standdown1969 by Charles R. Smith

[97]U. S. Marines in Vietnam High Mobility and Standdown1969 by Charles R. Smith

[98]U. S. Marines in Vietnam High Mobility and Standdown1969 by Charles R. Smith

[99]U. S. Marines in Vietnam High Mobility and Standdown1969 by Charles R. Smith

[100]http://www.marinemedals.com/morganwilliam.htm

[101]U. S. Marines in Vietnam High Mobility and Standdown1969 by Charles R. Smith

[102]Interview with Harvey Barnum

[103]Interview with Jay Standish, December 2017

[104]Interview with Jay Standish, January 2018

[105]http://www.historynet.com/vietnam-war-operation-dewey-canyon.htm

[106]U. S. Marines in Vietnam High Mobility and Standdown1969 by Charles R. Smith

[107]Documents supplied by Lt. Col. (ret.) James Loop

[108]Interview with Lt. Col. (ret.) James Loop, Memphis TN, June 14, 2014

[109]https://homeofheroes.com/silver-star/silver-star-vietnam-war/silver-star-vietnam-war-marines/silver-star-vietnam-war-marines-l/

[110]U. S. Marines in Vietnam High Mobility and Standdown1969 by Charles R. Smith

[111]U. S. Marines in Vietnam High Mobility and Standdown1969 by Charles R. Smith

[112]Interview with Harvey Barnum

[113]U. S. Marines in Vietnam High Mobility and Standdown1969 by Charles R. Smith

[114]U. S. Marines in Vietnam High Mobility and Standdown1969 by Charles R. Smith

[115]12th Marines Command Chronology March 1969; U. S. Marines in Vietnam High Mobility and Standdown1969 by Charles R. Smith

[116]U. S. Marines in Vietnam High Mobility and Standdown1969 by Charles R. Smith

[117]http://www.marinemedals.com/wilsonalfred.htm

[118]2nd Battalion, 12th Marines Command Chronology March, 1969; U. S. Marines in Vietnam High Mobility and Standdown1969 by Charles R. Smith

[119]U. S. Marines in Vietnam High Mobility and Standdown1969 by Charles R. Smith

[120]U. S. Marines in Vietnam High Mobility and Standdown1969 by Charles R. Smith

[121]U. S. Marines in Vietnam High Mobility and Standdown1969 by Charles R. Smith

[122]U. S. Marines in Vietnam High Mobility and Standdown1969 by Charles R. Smith

[123]U. S. Marines in Vietnam High Mobility and Standdown1969 by Charles R. Smith

ABOUT THE AUTHOR

Ronald E. Winter is the author of four books including the recently completed *Victory Betrayed, US Marines in Operation Dewey Canyon*. His other works include the non-fiction *Masters of the Art, A Fighting Marine's Memoir of Vietnam*, published by Random house, in addition to the non-fiction *Granny Snatching, How a 92-year-Old Widow Fought the Courts and Her Family to Win Her Freedom*, and *The Hypocrite*, his first novel, both published by Nightengale Press. He also has written more than a thousand magazine and newspaper articles. Winter joined the U. S. Marine Corps in January, 1966 serving four years on active duty including a 13-month tour in Vietnam as helicopter crewman, avionics technician and aerial gunner. He joined what was to become Marine Medium Helicopter Squadron (HMM)– 161 in October 1966 at the Marine Corps Air Station in New River, N.C., and stayed with that unit for more than two years.

While in Vietnam, in addition to his duties in avionics and flying "left seat" on test flights, Winter flew more than 300 missions as an aerial gunner, and was awarded 15 Air Medals, and Combat Aircrew wings with three stars. Winter flew for HMM-161 and HMM-164, both of which participated in Operation Dewey Canyon.

After returning stateside in June 1969 and completing his enlistment, Winter returned to college, earning undergraduate degrees in electrical engineering and English Literature.

After the Marines he spent nearly 20 years as a print journalist including stints as reporter, investigative reporter, supervising editor and columnist, earning numerous awards for investigative reporting, including a Pulitzer nomination. He has worked as an adjunct professor of communications, runs an event management business with his wife—specializing in military reunions—and is a certified personal trainer, as well as an amateur competitive power lifter. He also works as a media relations specialist for public relations, advertising, and marketing firms.

Acknowledgments

This work would not have been possible without the assistance, expertise and encouragement of a legion of participants who fought in Dewey Canyon or helped immeasurably in chronicling its historic importance many decades after the battle. Former Cpl. Joe Carcasio, HMM-161, provided invaluable research assistance, especially for the Tiger stories, and continued that support as the manuscript finally went to publication. John Robert Odom and Mike McElwee deserve special notice for their assistance. Thanks especially to Valerie Connelly for her publishing and editing expertise. Of particular note are the Dewey Canyon participants, the 9th Marines and their corpsmen, living and dead, who spent the better part of two months in an inhospitable environment, fighting a bitter enemy.

Also the 2nd Battalion, 12th Marines, the artillerymen who lived and fought alongside the "grunts," and in their own right made this all possible. The 2rd Battalion, 3rd Marines for their participation and sacrifices, the logistics troops at Vandegrift Combat Base and elsewhere, who showed that they, too, could be ingenious in their efforts, the communicators, dog handlers, as well as their canine counter-parts, engineers, and air crews who brought it all together at the outset, maintained it throughout the operation, and shut it all down at the end.

Individuals and publications who have kept the story of Dewey Canyon alive for decades: *Marine Rifleman: Forty-Three Years in the Corps,* by the late Col. Wesley L. Fox, *U.S. MARINES IN VIETNAM HIGH MOBILITY AND STANDDOWN 1969*, by Charles R. Smith, Leatherneck Magazine and the Marine Corps Gazette, *Green Hell,* by Beth Crumley, *SAPPER ATTACK ON FSB*

CUNNINGHAM by Michael Conroy, US Marine Rifleman in Vietnam 1965-73, by Charles Melson, and Cavalry of the Sky by the late Lynn Montross who provided historical perspective on Marine helicopter operations post-WWII and in the Korean War.

Individuals who participated in Operation Dewey Canyon including: the late Col. Wesley L. Fox, Lt. Miles Davis, Col. (ret.) Warren Wiedhahn, MGySgt. (ret.) Jack Payne, the late Lt. Col. James Loop, Col. (ret.) Joseph Snyder, Col. (ret.) Bo Honeycutt, Lt. John Cochenour, LCpl. Alan Sargent, Col. (ret.) Harvey "Barney" Barnum, Lt. Col. (ret.) John Wilkes, Lt. Col.(ret.) George Allen, Capt. Jay Standish, Cpl. Lewis Weber, Cpl. Tom "Quick Draw" McGraw, Capt. Gary Freese, Cpl. Ed Irwin, Cpl. Jeff Harnly, the late Cpl. Dan Haire, 1st Lt. Fred Penning, Major Fred Gatz, Lt. Col. (ret.) Dave White, Gen. (ret.) James McMonagle, SSgt. James Johnson, Capt. (USCG, Ret.) Bob Odom, LCpl Ed Oliver, LCpl Marco Polo Smigliani, HM2 Larry Sherer, John P. Murphy, Joe Carcasio.

In addition, Kevin B. Winter and Sharon Keane for their copy and content editing skills, Heather and Jennifer Winter for marketing and readability suggestions, and overall support.

Also, Jerry Clapper, Gladstone VFW Post #10906, Gladstone, MO, Michael and Linda Johnson, Tom (Marty) Martindale, John Glenn, Gene Massey, Glenn Baker, George Osborn, Byron Hill, Ray Cummings, Jay Boswell, Ed Egan, Hugh Holden, John Forlivio, Dave Longstreth, Tom Morrison, Ronnie Delaplain, Harry Howland, Gary Freese, Dale Bush, Louis Kern, Steve Stanick, Jim Chapin, Sheila Moore, Doug Davis, Richard Mueller, David White, Rena Minton, Zita Christian, Ron Balmer, Albert Hemingway, Harold Massey, Roger Gangi, Richard Latimer, Fred Penning, Lou Maupin, Charles Beasley, R. Lee, Tom Oliver, Ed Oliver, Roland Frech, David Dee Lawson, Lisa Cox, Ron Balmer, Bick DeMeo, David Allen, William Wittich, Jack Cress, Charles Heitkamp, Edward LeCouteur, Thomas Whitney, Frederick Somer.

And special thanks goes to the Marine Corps Heritage Foundation for supporting research about Operation Dewey Canyon.

MORE *by Ronald Winter*

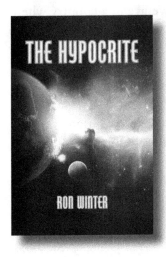

ISBN-13: 978-17348369-1-2
$19.95
Available from the author at
RonaldWinterBooks.com

Do bad genes move through the generations? Can the crimes done in one century be repeated hundreds of years later? Is a seed that is sown in the distant past, somehow able to send out shoots and runners so far into the future that no memory is left of the original transgression.

The Hypocrite is a celestial murder mystery, spanning the ages, and bringing two antagonists face-to-face in an environment that can only breed conflict. Bruce McAllister is a former Marine, recently returned from the fighting in Iraq where he served multiple tours. He survived myriad attacks and close calls as he made his way through cities and deserts his comrades nicknamed the Valley of the Shadow of Death.

He has returned home intact, in body and mind, but can he survive corporate America, in the person of Moran Smythe? And will McAllister survive working for The Hypocrite?

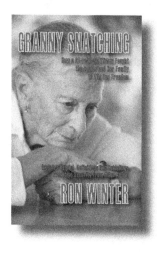

ISBN-13: 978-1933449838
$16.95
Available from the author at
RonaldWinterBooks.com and
on Amazon.com

It's safe to believe in the American Dream, isn't it? We live in a country where we take quality education, careers, nice homes, and the wherewithal to raise a family for granted.

We are well fed. We're warm. We keep up with the latest fashions. Our legal system provides swift justice and righteousness prevails. We solve problems, not create them! Right?

We anticipate a safe and secure retirement where we hold hands with our life's partner during leisurely strolls on golden sands - waving palms overhead and perfectly sized waves breaking on the shore beneath a glowing sunset. Each evening we are submerged in the warmth of a life lived long and well, and the promise that tomorrow will be just like today.

And then, KA-POW! Darkness falls upon us and our world is turned upside down as family members appear from nowhere, seizing us, dragging us toward an unanticipated and unwanted future, penniless, powerless, confined in the clutches of "elder care."

Unlikely? Think again. It happens every day all over America and it can happen to you. Is your future reasonably well planned out; ensuring that when you reach retirement age you will live the independent life you envisioned? Do you have a good lawyer who will help you navigate the uncharted waters of life for America's elderly ñ including proper care in case of illness or injury? Will your financial plans remain intact? Will you live as you hoped and planned for all those years with your family lovingly by your side?

Granny Snatching is an insidious creeping menace from which no one is safe. What nearly happened to Ella Winter can happen to you. Your life, like hers, can suddenly be thrown into chaos and disorder. Will you knuckle under or will you learn from her fight, and like Ella Winter stand tall and strong in the face of adversity.